FLAME

FLAME

The Story of My Mother Shahnaz Husain

NELOFAR CURRIMBHOY

First published in 2012 by Hachette India
(Registered name: Hachette Book Publishing India Pvt. Ltd)
An Hachette UK company
www.hachetteindia.com

1

Copyright © Nelofar Currimbhoy 2012
All pictures © Nelofar Currimbhoy 2012

Nelofar Currimbhoy asserts the moral right to be identified
as the proprietor of this work

ISBN 978-93-5009-469-3

Hachette Book Publishing India Pvt. Ltd
4th/5th Floors, Corporate Centre,
Plot no. 94, Sector 44, Gurgaon 122003, India

Typeset in Adobe Garamond 11/14.3
by InoSoft Systems Noida

Printed and bound in India by
Gopsons Papers Ltd., Noida

The Moving Finger writes; and having writ,
Moves on: nor all thy Piety nor Wit
Shall lure it back to cancel half a Line,
Nor all thy Tears wash out a Word of it.

So I, Nelofar Currimbhoy, dedicate this book
on my mother's life to the memory of my father
and set it free to the world.

Thanks, Tabrik, for being the love and anchor
in my life and for letting me keep the night lamp
on for three years;
Sharik, for being my friend always;
Zubek, for your intellect and wisdom – your insights appear so
often in this book;
And Mum – to you most of all – for living
the story of my book.

Prologue

I remember it as though it was yesterday; it is an image etched clearly in my mind. She is standing in front of the dresser, adjusting the large, three-piece mirror to see the back of her hair-do. The oval mirror with scalloped edges is a hand-me-down from her mother; I can even remember my grandmother's face gazing into it, when I was very young.

'How do I look?' she asks me, obviously pleased with the result, as she surveys her reflection. Her skin, like her mother's, is very white with a touch of rose but it is the luminosity of her eyes, sparkling in the mirror, that I remember most.

'I like you with your hair down, Mum,' I say. 'Won't you please wear it loose?'

She looks at me in the mirror. Her brows knit and a disconcerting frown appears – I should have said something else, I think, worried. Then she turns back to the mirror and with the flourish of a consummate artist pulls out the large black hair pins that hold her bouffant in place. Her long, lustrous hair cascades down her shoulders. I smile, delighted at the effect.

'Are you happy now?' she asks.

'Yes, Mum, your hair is so pretty left open. Why do you tie it up?' I say, pleased that she has agreed to my suggestion.

Flame

I watch as she combs her hair and makes a loose braid, her fingers weaving the locks that she flings casually behind her to swing down her back. From the corner of her eye she watches me, observing her intently. For a little girl it is simply magical to watch the transformation. She draws out her eyes in small fairy wings on the sides and then uses her favourite paler-than-pale lipstick. Her stretch tights are perfectly matched with a top in a flowing fabric; a pair of huge Go-Go glasses completes the effect. Then she turns for a last look in the mirror, seeking its approval; and when she smiles, the mirror says it all – she has always known how to artfully collaborate with it. And I fantasize that one day I will look just like her.

A sharp car horn startles us both and we dash to join my father who is waiting to drive us down to visit the new hotel in the city. The small red and white Standard Herald drives through the sparse roads of Delhi and heads towards the newest attraction in the city. The Oberoi Hotel has just opened its doors and will be, for many years to come, the most sought-after destination in the capital.

The coffee shop is the new hub; it smells of a mix of ground coffee beans, smoke and Chanel. The air buzzes with the chatter of groups that remain tucked on the loungers for hours as the coffee-machine whirls constantly, only the click of high-heeled shoes cutting through the hum. As we walk into the icy cool lobby we spot a good-looking couple surrounded by a crowd of awestruck onlookers. It is the young and handsome Nawab of Pataudi, the cricket hero and his begum, the gorgeous celluloid star Sharmila Tagore. My mother is excited at spotting the celebrities and twists her head and peers to catch a better glimpse. She has never seen any superstars before and this is a dream come true.

This is the story of my mother who was born a flame, a flame so bright that not all of life's storms could douse a single spark of her intensely free spirit. Every time a wave splashed on her, she rose again with an irrepressible energy – the energy of life and passion. How else would you explain the path she steered her life through?

Her incredible journey is perhaps best explained in the opening words of one of her more memorable talks:

'I was born to a traditional Muslim family, I was engaged at fourteen and married at sixteen; I had my first child within a year and today I am speaking to you at Harvard after attending President Obama's summit of world entrepreneurs in Washington D.C.

'I had dreams of going to college as a young girl but that was not possible for me. People go to college at the beginning of their careers; I have got here after a lifetime of success and achievements. I am here as a student and a speaker at the same time.

'Would I have done it any better if I had come to Harvard at sixteen? I am not sure if I would have but I am sure of one thing – I would not have wished my career to be any different. Strangely, I have found that almost everything that was taught to me in my course, I have already applied over the years.

'Perhaps, I was simply fortified with business instincts.'

With her quintessential abilities, my mother Shahnaz Husain has risen to become one of India's foremost businesswomen – a glamorous personality, a formidable competitor to every multinational that has entered the country – and yet she has remained a strongly traditional woman; her personal life effortlessly entwining with her professional life to make her the woman she is. She has lived her life like a tight-rope artist, balancing her deeply ingrained family values with an impulse to succeed; or perhaps it was the flame within that drove her from the complacency that comes with early marriage, to arrive at heights that few can scale.

My mother is my idea of a complete woman; to me, a complete woman is one who, while exploring her intellect and her talents, visits all the facets of her femininity with the same intensity and passion. Perhaps it is because of her demanding lifestyle that she gives herself the respect and care that Nature expects. She pays her dues to life by saying, 'You have given me a gift in this wonderful body and I, in return, will treasure it.'

I have seen her waking up at four in the morning to do her henna workout before catching an early morning flight. The famed mane is worked on with devotion with a formula of twelve eggs, curd and an herb-enriched oil that gives it its auburn sheen. She has no patience with women who neglect their appearance citing the common refrain: 'I have no time.'

'There is *always* time if you have the *will* to look beautiful,' she maintains.

Her day starts with a cup of herbal tea with honey and lemon. After an hour-long session of yoga and meditation it is time for her hairdresser and make-up artist to come in. They take a quick glance at her day's schedule to check whether their boss has to face the camera; the make-up they use would need to be altered for the arc lights. The containers on her table are all colour-coded and organized. The mascaras, liners and foundations are in distinct sections. Her personal favourites from her product range – creams, lotions, oils and packs – are stacked to a side along with the new entrants that are used personally by her before they go onto the shelves – only *after* she has assured herself that they meet her exacting standards. Her meticulous nature is quite evident in this very personal space of hers – a space in which, perhaps, this is the first time there has been such a close intrusion.

Aware of the ticking clock, she sips her breakfast from small glasses of assorted raw vegetable juices. A cup of nuts, seeds and raisins, some papaya, apple and slices of boiled egg-white complete the power recipe that will take her through the day; a couple of capsules of concentrated herbs provide the right balance of Nature's resources. She then starts making her calls, normally to the factories and to her secretary to plan out her day and, of course, there is the habitual morning call to me. By the time she is ready she has put in an hour of work.

She usually decides what she is going to wear before she starts her make-up, so the accessories are pulled out by the staff and kept ready for her to choose from. In my mother's world, accessories contribute a major part in the perfectly-turned-out look. Her wardrobe is stored in open racks and resembles an haute couture store in its dazzling array of never-ending textures and colours, studded with diamantes and lined with trimmings. The collection is dotted with creations of the finest fashion houses – Dior, Lagerfeld, Rohit Bal and Tarun Tahiliani rub shoulders with a host of others but in the end, what dominates her wardrobe is her unique personality, the signature Shahnaz Husain style. It is there, stamped on her tall heeled shoes, her flowing kaftans or, of late, her coats, her rings and jewellery, which she wears more as fashion accessories and for effect rather than for their value. She inspects herself in the mirror one last time and when she steps out she does so with the confidence that she looks stunning.

The kind of people that she will meet in a day are foreign buyers, who would, in all probability, have taken long flights to come to meet her; press and television crews; students and clients keen on meeting her personally. For all of them, for those who have been drawn across the miles with an image in their minds, for her staff and for her family, she has made sure that she will not disappoint.

For those who have never had the opportunity of meeting my mother I can only say I have tried to describe her but I am not sure I can. Ideally, I would like to take a paintbrush and draw her on a canvas, simply because she is so visual but then there would be so much missing; I would want to take her favourite fragrance 'Angel' by Thierry Mugler and spray it on the painting and yet there would be something missing. As I once told a reporter, 'She is an aura. How do I describe an aura?'

All these years later, when I sit down to write about her, a tangible description still eludes me. She is an energy who embodies the elements, as you shall discover in this, her story, told as no one else can. I was there, by her side, at every moment. I have walked her journey with her and watched her life unfold like the saga of a storybook.

The silence in the Ronald Reagan Hall is palpable as rows of delegates from sixty countries wait for the man on whose invitation they are here on a perfect April evening in Washington D.C. All at once, the ubiquitous appearance of security-men smoothly fills the hall and is followed by a presence that is all-pervasive. A commanding voice breaks through the tacit stillness; it is deep and strong and bears the hallmark of an intensity of purpose.

'Let me, on behalf of the American people, say welcome to the United States of America.'

President Obama is present in person to honour and appreciate the best and the brightest entrepreneurs of the world. The chosen few have been selected by a high-level committee that includes Secretary of State, Hillary Clinton. The mostly male audience is dressed in formal perfectly cut suits, except for the representative from India – a glamorous looking lady with striking long red hair, dressed in a black kaftan with Swarovski embellishments – a stark, stunning contrast, in the staid atmosphere. She represents not just herself but all Indian women and their ability to achieve. She represents the ability of her country to allow its citizens that freedom and opportunity.

President Obama continues: 'I want to thank you for being part of this historic event. You're visionaries who have pioneered new industries.'

The lady's eyes grow moist, overwhelmed as she is by the President's compelling rhetoric. She feels moved by the moment; by this moment of recognition that is beyond material success and she knows that she has reached the pinnacle of her career as an internationally acknowledged personality.

'We've come together today because of what we share – a belief that we are all bound together by certain common aspirations: To live with dignity. To get an education. To live healthy lives. Maybe to start a business, without having to pay a bribe to anybody. To speak freely and have a say in how we are governed. To live in peace and security and to give our children a better future.'

The President's words, powerful and inspirational, float through the huge space; it seems to her that he is speaking only to her. Tonight is special in so many ways. To be a guest at President Obama's Summit of World Entrepreneurs is to be honoured by a man who is a physical embodiment of the 'dream-come-true' to the millions who trusted Martin Luther King's moving words, 'I have a dream that one day...' – a visionary himself who has achieved the unthinkable and now leads by example.

'So this is the incredible potential that you represent, the future we can seize together.'

There is thunderous applause as the delegates stand up to honour the man whose election campaign, 'Yes, we can', has become an inspiration for many that fight to reach out to seemingly impossible goals.

The representative from India leaves the hall holding his words in her mind. The long black limousine she rides in glides down

Pennsylvania Avenue, resplendent with the cherry-blossom blooms that shine luminous in the halogen lights.

The next few days are spent indulging in true American-style hospitality that has been meticulously planned for the delegates and is unsparingly extravagant. The nights are filled with galas and dinners and the days with talks and meetings with business groups.

The international press has been observing the delegates and there is more than a mild curiosity in the charismatic lady from India. Who is she? What brought her to this summit? The questions are never-ending.

Today, when I go shopping with my mother it is hard to get past the crowds who push forward bits of paper, scrap-books, sometimes even their bare hands, to get an autograph of Shahnaz Husain, India's reigning beauty queen, the head of a homespun beauty empire entirely of her own making. I step back and smile, watching her glide down the aisles of the mall with her mane of red hair crowning her head, commanding instant recognition and attention from onlookers. How little she knew of the future back then, of the stars that she carried in her own book of life, of her own impending super-stardom.

I was right. I always *did* like Mum with her hair down.

A Star Is Born

If, in life, we are to be judged by what we make of ourselves, we must also acknowledge that there is another side to us, where we live our lives with the genes we inherit; the traits our ancestors hand down to us are the building blocks on which our destinies are formed.

To know Shahnaz Husain as we see her today and wonder where they make women like her, her ancestry, I think, would be an appropriate place to start; an interesting way of getting to know her better.

The fifth of November was like any other day. The impending birth of one more grandchild at Rahat Manzil did not create undue consternation in the stately mansion. The child waiting to be born would be the youngest of three – the eldest being a sister Malika, followed by a brother, Walliullah.

Her father, Nasirullah Beg, was the son of the Chief Justice of Hyderabad and her mother, Sayeeda Begum was the daughter of the Commander-in-Chief of the Hyderabad Army; the third successive generation to hold that position. The wedding of her parents was the result of an alliance between the two leading families of Hyderabad, arranged personally by the Nizam who wanted to see the children of his Chief Justice and the

Commander-in-Chief of his army united in marriage. Perhaps, the Nizam, in all his wisdom, had intended, in a subconscious part of his mind – before the days of 'genetic engineering' – to unite the gene pools of the two most enigmatic families of Hyderabad.

Sayeeda Begum's petite, almost frail body felt weighed down by her nine-month pregnancy as she looked out of a window from the privacy of her room, onto the never-ending grounds of Rahat Manzil – the palatial home where she had grown up. Her mind went back to the days when her father Nawab Osman Yar Ud Daulah was alive and she used to peep out of the window with girlish admiration as his entourage entered the gates.

She gazed out onto the sprawling grounds and could see herself, once more a twelve-year-old, in breeches and boots, playing polo in purdah. The women's polo field at Rahat Manzil was a popular venue for the young aristocratic girls of the time, who came draped modestly in veils and then seamlessly stepped into polo gear and mounted the finest of horses. Holding mallets in their delicate hands the women of Rahat Manzil rode proudly in their saddles, equalling their brothers in every aspect.

The unconventional traditions and culture of Rahat Manzil had been etched out by its flag-bearer, Sayeeda's grandfather, Sir Afsar Ul Mulk. He was a rebel of his times, a man who believed in the empowerment of women – of the girls in his family handling swords and roses with the same ease – because Sir Afsar had the foresight to know that they would face many adversities in life and handling these situations with courage was something he wished to ensure they would be adept at.

The young Sayeeda had been taught how to wield a sword at a very early age, in fact, for the girls of Rahat Manzil sword-fencing was a mandatory sport. She also remembered herself, then not more than four, being taken with the other children in the family to play with tiger cubs so that they would learn to be brave and fearless.

Her eyes smiled as she reminisced about her spectacular childhood in her parents' home. Just then her mother, Amina – as she was called by her family – entered the room. A delicate lady with a gentle voice, she was the last lady of the house at Rahat Manzil. Walking up to her daughter she asked, 'How do you feel?' with concern. Sayeeda turned back, holding her stomach and Amina knew the moment she looked at her daughter's face that it was time to call for the doctor.

Nasirullah paced up and down before the closed doors of a room that had been converted into a private delivery chamber. Not one to give in to anxiety, he prayed under his breath for his wife and the child they were yet to see. His father, Mirza Samiullah Beg, was a highly-respected man and the Chief Justice of Hyderabad. One of the few men of his time to be educated at Cambridge, Samiullah had in turn sent his sons to England to study law at his alma mater and had the satisfaction of seeing them both become Chief Justices during his lifetime. Nasirullah went on to become the Chief Justice of Uttar Pradesh, while Hamidullah, his younger brother, was appointed the Chief Justice of India. Interestingly, Samiullah was also amongst the first to acquire a car in Hyderabad. When he drove out in the open-top marvel, sitting in the rear seat, people kneeled in fear thinking he was some kind of divine incarnation.

Although Samiullah Beg held a key position in the government, he remained a strong supporter of the freedom movement. He made his intolerance of British rule quite public by refusing to stand up when the viceroy entered a function and then dramatically walking out after a while. Motilal Nehru – a personal friend – was always welcome in the Chief Justice's home. When the freedom movement was at its peak, the British government sent a letter to him, accusing him of compromising his position as Chief Justice by allowing his residence to be used for anti-government activities and demanding that he immediately stop giving refuge to Motilal Nehru, whom they claimed was using Beg's home as a hideout. Samiullah is said to have sent a stern reply to the governor, saying, 'Motilal is my friend and my doors will always remain open for him.' If the British government had any objection to him hosting his friend, he stated, he was willing to resign; Samiullah was known for his principled stand on issues and was deeply respected for it.

When Nasirullah finished his education, news of his return from Cambridge spread quickly through the upper echelons in India. It was a time when the combination of aristocracy and a good British education was rare and offers for employment began pouring in for the young man from various parts of the country. Samiullah Beg, however, was in favour of his son returning to Lucknow and starting his law practice there. Though his ancestors were deposed royals of Samarkand, he had been born in Lucknow and had left behind a string of magnificent properties when he had moved to Hyderabad. He now expressed his eagerness to see his elder son return to the family's roots. 'You could try it out,' he said. 'And you can always return to Hyderabad should you choose to.'

My grandfather agreed to move to Lucknow and soon realized that the low-key town was better suited to his tastes than the hedonistic lifestyle of Hyderabad. In the years that followed, Lucknow was to become his natural home, where he lived with Sayeeda and their three children.

The train journey from Hyderabad to Lucknow was long and tedious for the young Nasirullah and his new bride. As they scaled the arid countryside, Nasirullah's eyes kept returning to the black garb that his wife had now folded neatly and set aside. He remembered her snowy-white skin glistening under the black chiffon veil as she had climbed on to the train and the thought of the dark fabric stifling her face upset him. Would it be wrong to take away what she considered a symbol of her modesty? Was purdah a part of her culture? He debated in silence. Finally the decision seemed clear – freedom was not a choice but a right he wanted his wife to have and if her conditioning did not allow her to free herself from the shackles that had now become a habit, he would break those barriers for her.

With a flourish, he lifted the burqa and flung it out of the moving train, setting his wife's beautifully chiselled face free forever.

Now Nasirullah waited for news outside the room at Rahat Manzil where his wife was in the final stages of labour. Sayeeda, being the most patient of women, barely displayed any signs of the great pain she was in, other than taking Allah's name under her breath. When the door finally opened, the doctor emerged, smiling.

'Congratulations, Mr Beg! It is a girl.'

Nasirullah's parents, Samiullah Beg and his wife, arrived to see and bless their newborn granddaughter. Samiullah looked at her and softly said, 'Shahnaz' – the favourite child of the king – as though it were a blessing.

The name became the most accurate of prophecies, because as she grew older, Shahnaz became her father's darling.

Holding Mummy's Hand

Sayeeda Begum escorted her youngest daughter Shahnaz to the La Martinière College in Lucknow for her first day at school on a hot summer's day. The magnificent structure, built on the banks of the river Gomti in Lucknow, was a bastion of the British at the time and Shahnaz was one of the few Indian students in its privileged environs. Holding her mother's hand, she looked around, a trifle perplexed, wondering why all the children had blond hair.

When Shahnaz ran out of the school gates later that afternoon – a little concerned that she might have been abandoned forever – she beamed a relieved smile to see her mother waiting for her in the sun, a sleek clutch in her hand, the edge of her crisp cotton sari elegantly covering her head. Shahnaz jumped happily with her into the waiting car.

They drove through the sleepy afternoon streets of Lucknow and stopped in front of a three-storeyed mansion. Marble House, situated in the heart of Lucknow, was the family home of the Begs. The building had been constructed by a British jeweller who had decided to return to England. It had been bought by the Begs with its accompanying estate of a row of shops and a small gated compound of twenty-odd homes.

Shahnaz tore up the familiar stairs and ran through the maze of rooms. It was the perfect house to play hide-and-seek in with her brother Wally because it had more than fifty rooms. She arranged her schoolbooks neatly on her table and waited for the evening, when she could show them off to her doting father.

The young Shahnaz settled into school life with ease. She had begun to enjoy her time at school and so remembers all the more vividly the moment when the blissful days of her childhood came crashing rudely to the ground. She clearly remembers the day because her life changed irrevocably.

She had noticed her mother looking a little pale for some time now. She no longer went for her ritual evening walks and instead of finding her waiting at the lunch table when she got back from school, Shahnaz was often told in a hushed voice, 'Mummy is sleeping because she is tired.' The children were dismayed to find doctors visiting the house regularly and wondered what was wrong.

Shahnaz being the youngest never strayed far from her mother. On that particular day she was hidden behind the door, peering into the living room where Dr Merchant, the British lady doctor who was treating Sayeeda Begum, was explaining her worsening condition to her father.

'She is suffering from tuberculosis of the lungs. Unfortunately, there is no complete cure. Penicillin will only slow down the inevitable and contain the disease so it will not be contagious.'

'How long do I have?' asked Sayeeda Begum abruptly.

'Well, it depends…' Dr Merchant began evasively but at the look in her patient's eyes she admitted, 'Anywhere up to three years.'

Seeing the serious expression on her parents' faces, Shahnaz began to sob and ran down the corridor to her brother's room.

'Mummy is going to *die*, I just heard the doctor. She said Mummy is going to *die!*' the little girl wept helplessly.

The environment in the house changed drastically from that day on, as though a pall of gloom had fallen over it. The children went about the house looking shaken and scared. Shahnaz, the youngest, sobbed a lot. Her older brother, consoling her without success, became her closest friend and support at this point. The living room was converted into a sanatorium-like area for their mother and the children were forbidden from entering it. They gathered around the window and watched her through the glass barrier with concern and deep fear.

One night, Shahnaz dreamt her mother was being carried by angels into the clouds. She woke up from her sleep and spent the next few hours sobbing and praying. It pains me even after so many years to think of my mother facing one of life's biggest challenges at an age when little girls fall asleep listening to fairy-tales.

Sayeeda Begum was deeply religious and spent her days immersed in prayer. Not all the training on the polo fields, or the sword-fencing duels, or her years at Rahat Manzil, however, had prepared her to face her young children and see the stark fear in their eyes. She felt as though she had betrayed her family, yet there was very little she could do about her deteriorating health. Dr Merchant was doing the best she could and after a few weeks of taking penicillin, Sayeeda Begum was declared non-contagious. In those dark times, the moment came like a ray of hope and the children rushed to her wildly. She looked at young Shahnaz and smiled. 'Chhoti Baby, I will not die till I have got you married,' she promised.

Nasirullah Beg was a deeply tormented man; he shared every moment of his wife's pain. Being one of the leading lawyers of his time, with commitments to clients, he struggled to balance work and his children. It was then that my mother's first cousin, Meher Apa, came to stay with the family and for the next two years enveloped the children in her warmth and love. The young girl cared for them, took them on special outings and made them laugh, helping them forget their pain for a while.

Meher Apa has a very special place in my mother's life and to this day she regards her with the deepest affection. Meher Apa tried to cheer her little cousins with every possible distraction. The children visited the Residency gardens in Lucknow almost every evening. One day, during the beginning of spring, when the garden was brimming with flowers, they saw a beautiful golden cocker spaniel bounding down the path with an old British gentleman holding her leash. Jenny spotted the children and ran up to them, wagging her tail and displaying a spontaneous affection. It was as though she understood their pain and was trying to cheer them up.

The children were thrilled when what started off as a chance encounter in the park became a daily ritual. Every evening the children would take biscuits and titbits for Jenny to the park where Mr Little, the dog's owner and she would be waiting for them.

On one such evening a few months later, Mr Little looked preoccupied. 'I am planning to return home to England and I can't think of giving Jenny to anyone other than you all. Do you think you could keep her, please?' he asked.

Shahnaz held her breath in disbelief as did Wally and Malika. 'We would love to keep Jenny,' they finally announced.

'You should check with your family first,' smiled Mr Little.

The next day, the children arrived at the park with their father, who was keen to meet the delightful Jenny who had brought so much happiness into the lives of his children.

'She will be no trouble. She is a good girl,' Mr Little tried convincing Justice Beg.

Jenny was wagging her tail and looking into his face as though begging him to agree. Nasirullah needed little persuasion. 'Yes,' he said immediately. 'We will keep Jenny.'

The children were overjoyed. Mr Little bent down and hugged his dog for one last time and then he walked away without looking back, sad but secure in the knowledge that she was in good hands.

Jenny brought a sense of playfulness to the sombre atmosphere in Marble House and Sayeeda Begum smiled as she saw her children giggling with joy after a long time as the sprightly dog went from room to room familiarizing herself with her new home. At least, she thought, the new pet had succeeded in distracting them from the fact that her condition was worsening by the day.

Two years had passed since Sayeeda had taken ill and the prognosis was not encouraging. Dr Merchant warned Nasirullah that his wife's condition was deteriorating fast and strongly recommended that he admit her to a sanatorium in Kasauli, which in those years was the best facility in the country for the ailment.

'If you try to keep her at home any longer, you will reduce her chances of recovery,' she warned.

Being able to see his wife every day had been a source of great comfort for Nasirullah. Sending her to a sanatorium seemed like the first step towards losing her but it was clear now that the doctor's advice could no longer be ignored. So it was with a heavy heart that he told the children that their mother was leaving them to stay in a place where she would become better.

Since his hectic schedule as a lawyer did not leave him much time to look after his three young children, it was decided that they would be admitted to the La Martinière boarding school and that Meher Apa would return to Hyderabad to continue her college education. The children understood the crisis the family was facing and agreed without a fuss but they had one condition: Jenny would be brought down to visit them as often as possible.

Their father promised them this, knowing how much they loved their dog.

My mother remembers putting her most precious belongings into a suitcase – her favourite doll Maggie, her frilly dresses and her colouring books – packing her bag to leave home at the age of six. She felt very grown up and responsible that day. In fact, she had matured far beyond her age in those troubled years. The three children said goodbye to their mother and sat in the car with their father, holding each other's hands, afraid and unsure of the future.

Little Shahnaz stood on the seat and watched her mother till she became a haze of tears in her eyes.

Boarding School

The Shahnaz Husain who would emerge years later as a fighter – determined and spirited – was born partly in the very early years spent at boarding school where loneliness and the instinct for survival chiselled aspects of her personality.

La Martinière was a missionary school and like all convents, the emphasis on religious education was strong. Nuns in stiff white robes stood out in their austere clothing as a reminder of the religiosity and principles of the institution. Every day, a class was reserved for Biblical teachings. While rows of girls lined up to go to class, Shahnaz sat alone. Deeply concerned that the child might grow up lost and faithless, Sister Francis, the headmistress, invited Nasirullah Beg for a discussion.

'Mr Beg,' she said. 'As you know, we are a Christian school and we have no teachings in Islam. I suggest you make some arrangements for a teacher to come in so Shahnaz can learn about her religion.'

Nasirullah Beg smiled at the headmistress gently and said, 'Sister, since I am unable to teach her my faith, you might as well teach her yours.'

Touched by his words, Sister Francis watched the tall man walk out of the room having challenged the boundaries of all faiths, secure in the belief that her God would be as good for his child as his own.

Boarding school was not like home and the young Shaina – as she was called by her British classmates – no longer had the luxury of fussing over her food, or to sometimes revel in the freedom of leaving her meals halfway and running off to play chased by a hysterical maid. Those days – when her mother's only preoccupation was to feed her and hers was to get away from the tyranny of force-feeding – had ended abruptly.

Now food was sacred and tuck from home a precious commodity; sharing with the dozens of little girls who were her dormitory mates became a necessary survival instinct and occasional diplomacy at age seven a tactic that came with existing in an alien environment with new people.

Tuck, as I said, was very precious and sharing with your dorm-mates a strict rule. Whenever Shahnaz would open her bottle of jam or nibble at a chocolate she would make it a point to politely offer it to her neighbours who would happily accept it.

It was here in those days of struggle that Shahnaz faced her first lesson of life. Once, Nasirullah Beg went out of town on work and the man who was meant to deliver the children's food package did not arrive. Shahnaz and Malika stared at the long driveway all day, waiting anxiously but there was no sign of anyone. In the evening, Shahnaz watched her friends tear through their packages in their excitement to get to the goodies inside.

'Aren't you going to share your jam with me?' she asked Helen who sat comfortably on her bed, eating strawberry jam with bread.

'No way,' said Helen.

Shahnaz sat patiently, hurt and upset and then she decided to do the unthinkable. She got her spoon, dashed towards Helen's table, where the jar was left open, dipped deep into the bottle and ran – the object of her desire safely in her mouth before anyone could move.

There was mayhem; there had been a jam robbery and the headmistress was informed of the indiscretion. Nasirullah Beg was summoned to the school to reprimand his daughter, whom the headmistress called a difficult and uncontrollable child. As he sat looking across the table at the fuming and formidable Sister, his daughter stood demurely by, her hands behind her back in true missionary-school style.

He bent down to her and asked, 'Why did you take away your friend's jam, Shahnaz?'

'I got tempted, Papa,' candidly confessed the young Shahnaz. 'I always share my tuck with Helen but last Sunday my tuck did not come; I had nothing to eat and she refused to share her jam with me.'

Nasirullah Beg was nonplussed. The man who presided over some of the thorniest trials in court, for once, had to reserve his judgement.

Despite her trials at boarding school, my mother has very fond memories of her time at La Martinière. One of her best friends at school was a girl called Elizabeth de Cruz. Lizzie was a sensitive and warm-hearted girl and she and Shahnaz became close friends and remained so throughout their boarding-school days. Elizabeth's cousin, Neville Fleming, went to La Martinière Boys' School and visited her on Sundays. It wasn't long before the now seven-year-old Shahnaz with her luxurious curls and large brown eyes caught his attention and the ten-year-old was smitten. It took several visits before he finally expressed his feelings through Elizabeth. 'Neville says you are very beautiful, Shaina. I think he loves you.' Once news of Neville's crush spread in the dormitory the much-awaited Sundays came to be known as 'Neville Fleming days'.

Shahnaz worked hard at her lessons and struggled to remain ahead in class. She faced the challenge of competing with girls who had their parents to support them in their studies at home and she often heard the words 'Mummy helped me with this lesson' and felt a dip of sadness in her heart. She also had a natural flair for dramatics and was confident and expressive on stage. The school was quick to realize that the child was gifted in many ways and they made sure that she was encouraged with opportunities to develop her talents.

It was the time of the year when the school put up its best act and opened its doors to parents to show itself off as the perfect place for their children to be. The annual day at La Martinière was an important occasion and that year the highlight of the celebration included a Red Indian dance. The lights in the sprawling auditorium had been dimmed and the stage looked like an illuminated fish-tank. The audience looked on expectantly as the silence was broken by the loud beat of drums. Shahnaz, dressed as a Native American chief with a crown of multicoloured feathers on her head, appeared on stage leading her tribe of Red Indians who carefully followed her every move in a train-like formation. Halfway through the performance, Shahnaz felt the elastic holding up her trousers snap. Not one to accept defeat or leave the stage, she astutely used the arm movements of the dance to keep her pants up from each side in turn. Trained to follow their leader, the junior dancers also began to copy her and soon the hall was roaring with applause for the brave child who managed to complete the entire performance and showed that she had in her the qualities of a leader and a fighter.

Around this time, Nasirullah Beg, who had become one of the most prominent lawyers in Lucknow, was offered the position of Judge of the Allahabad High Court. The new appointment suited Nasirullah's temperament and though the prospect of moving home without Sayeeda by his side was daunting he accepted it immediately. He travelled frequently between the two cities in the process of shifting homes and it was on one of his journeys to Allahabad that he decided to take Jenny along with him. She sat happily beside him, enjoying the rocking of the train, peering out of the window at every stop. When the train stopped at the small rural town of Nawabganj, Justice Beg glanced at his watch; it was 6pm, the perfect time for a quick evening stroll. As he was getting off, Jenny looked at him, wagging her tail excitedly. It seemed that, like her master, she too was longing to stretch her legs. Justice Beg gave in and leashed her. They walked up and down the deserted station in the light of the setting sun until the stationmaster's whistle announced that the journey was about to resume. Justice Beg quickly walked back to the door of his compartment but as he was climbing the steps, the huge wheels of the locomotive began to churn. The deafening sound grew louder each moment. Plumes of steam gushed out of the engines while Jenny stood frozen with fear, afraid to move any closer. Justice Beg watched as the leash slipped out of his hands. 'Come on, Jenny, come on,' he called helplessly as Jenny broke into a desperate run before stopping and looking back at him, defeated and confused.

Justice Beg managed to stop the train and returned to Nawabganj station in search of Jenny but by then she was nowhere to be seen.

On Sunday morning Shahnaz and Malika woke up early and got dressed in anticipation of their father's visit. On his last visit, he had promised that he would bring Jenny with him. After taking turns at smothering her with hugs and kisses, they would always sit down in some peaceful spot and regale him with the week's happenings and give him the list of goodies that they wanted on his next visit. It was a day that they looked forward to but this Sunday, Justice Beg had a knot in his stomach as he waited to see his children.

'What is the matter, Papa?' asked Wally when he saw the troubled look on his father's face. 'Is Mummy okay?'

'Mummy is fine but I have to give you some bad news.' He didn't have to say another word.

'Where is Jenny?' they asked at the same time.

'I am so sorry to have to tell you this but I lost her at the Nawabganj station,' said Justice Beg barely looking up.

The children's eyes brimmed over with tears. Jenny was not just a pet, she was the angel who took away their grief at boarding-school and made each lonely week easier. Sundays were never the same again because they were a reminder of a friend who no longer would come to meet them.

On a balmy evening a few months later, Justice Beg was enjoying one of his last few walks in the Residency gardens before finally moving to Allahabad when he suddenly spotted a golden cocker spaniel sitting under a banyan tree in the distance. As he went closer he gasped in disbelief. It was Jenny! Guided by an instinct beyond human comprehension she had made it back to the place where Mr Little used to bring her to meet the children every day. Justice Beg walked towards her eagerly. The little dog stood up, feeble from her long journey. As she limped up to him, Justice Beg noticed that she was thin and very ill. Jenny wagged her tail slowly, licked him profusely and then laid her head on his feet and shut her eyes forever.

17

My mother still cannot talk of Jenny without tears in her eyes and I have heard about her so often that at times she seems to be mine too, in some strange way.

Life is a continual journey – never-ending, ever-changing – and the belief that nothing lasts forever is as true of pain as it is of joy. When the children were mourning the loss of Jenny in the loneliness of their boarding school, there came an unexpected surprise. One evening, just as they were sitting down for their evening tea and biscuits the warden summoned them to the visitors' room. Standing near a window, in the glow of the evening light, was their mother, looking as beautiful as an angel. Their father stood by with a broad smile. The room echoed with unrestrained joy as Sayeeda Begum bent down to embrace her children, sobbing with happiness at finally being reunited with them. There is no love that is like a mother's and never a moment when this was truer.

The House on Stanley Road

The two-storeyed house at 33 Stanley Road stood on the banks of the Ganges in Allahabad. On full-moon nights the waters glistened in luminous ripples and cast a soft glow on the creeper-laden walls. There was a sense of calm about the house, as though its empty spaces were waiting to be filled with warmth; to finally become a home.

The young children jumped out of the car with their mother and a beaming father, their world filled with happiness once more, their minds at peace. The reunited family had overcome the days of uncertainty and despair and had returned home together. Mrs Beg had fought her illness bravely and they had overcome their trials. The simplest joys that they had always taken for granted now seemed like a gift from the heavens, a gift snatched away and returned.

Nooran, the nanny, was beside herself with excitement as she hugged each of the children. '*Mere pyaare bacche,*' she cried, holding them tight. It was an overwhelming moment and one that my mother will always remember as her most precious, her most sacred.

Inside the house, the table tops were being polished, the rooms cleaned twice over and flowers placed in vases that remained empty. The cook was busy in the kitchen, making the children's favourite dishes and adding an extra special garnish for good measure. The lady of the house had returned and the relief showed on every person's face.

My grandmother walked around the house like a queen reclaiming her domain, her eyes scanning every detail to see how her home had managed without her. After all, the house had been shifted from Lucknow to Allahabad without her supervision. She checked the curtains for dust, she peered into her china cupboard to see if it was all safe and intact and then she went to her room and spread her prayer mat and thanked God for the blessings she had received. How strange it is that we ask God for what we perceive as the big things in life, while we forget that, in fact, it is the smallest things that are the most important – that you wake up in the morning and have your loved ones around you; that you can walk on both your legs; that you have your health. I am sure each one of us would happily give up the crown jewels for these priceless blessings.

In Allahabad, Shahnaz and Malika were admitted to St. Mary's Convent while Wally joined the boys' high school. On their first day at their new school they waited eagerly for the last bell to ring. The thought that they would not be eating a lunch of stew and rolled chapattis on a long wooden table with benches in the dining hall was gratifying.

Sure enough, when they returned home their mother was waiting at an elegantly set table laden with her children's favourite dishes. She intended to spoil them for days to come; it was her way of making up for her long absence.

In the years that followed, Shahnaz excelled in her studies, working hard to maintain her status as the best student in her class, ahead of her arch rival in academics, Diptima Mukerjee.

However Kimmy Malhotra, the daughter of a professor, was Shahnaz's rival in personality. One day, on the play-field, Kimmy walked up to Shahnaz and pushed her. Shahnaz stared at her in shock wondering how to deal with the situation. Then her eyes moved to Kimmy's two long plaits that hung temptingly in front of Shahnaz. She grabbed at them with both her hands. Kimmy shrieked in pain and then retaliated by grabbing Shahnaz's mop of hair. But her hair was short and in a few seconds Kimmy's hold slipped free. Shahnaz, still holding her plaits, didn't quite know what to do next and then they both burst out laughing uncontrollably. Somehow that broke the ice for them forever and they became the best of friends for years to come.

The writer in Shahnaz was also emerging and her way with words ensured that she gradually acquired the position of the resident playwright at St. Mary's.

One day, Shahnaz handed in a skit she had written. 'Shahnaz,' said Mrs Misra the next morning. 'This is an excellent piece of work.'

'Thank you, Madam,' said Shahnaz.

'The character of the queen is quite dramatic.'

'Thank you, Madam. It is very strong.'

'And who did you have in mind for that role, Shahnaz?'

Shahnaz looked down, a little embarrassed. 'I would like to play the part, Madam, if you permit me.'

Mrs Misra looked at Shahnaz through the bifocals perched on the tip of her nose. 'Did you write this role for yourself?'

'Yes, Madam,' confessed Shahnaz.

Mrs Misra looked amused, a small smile creasing her face. 'Really? Are you sure you can play this part?'

Shahnaz nodded eagerly.

Mrs Misra could not question her spirit. 'You are very confident, Shahnaz, very sure of yourself. Okay, the role is yours.'

Shahnaz burst out of Mrs Misra's room, announcing to everyone she encountered in a thrilled voice: 'I am the queen! I am the queen!'

The play was a success and Shahnaz's performance as the queen – complete with a glittering cardboard tiara and flowing gown – left Mrs Misra speechless. Grandeur, it seemed, came naturally to this young girl.

Shahnaz's relationships with her brother and sister also took shape in these years and it became clear that Wally and she shared a strong bond. Her lively nature found an affinity with her brother's; she preferred playing ninepins and marbles with him over spending time with Malika, who was quieter and kept mostly to herself.

Shahnaz and Malika were as far apart in temperament as any two sisters could ever be. Malika considered Shahnaz unruly and messy and she often showed her disapproval of her younger sister's behaviour. Malika's priorities were different – she was very particular about her clothes being neat and well-ironed, her room remained spick and span and she had a complete intolerance for any lack of hygiene. When evening tea was put out for the family the piece de résistance was the scrumptious assortment of freshly baked pastries that were personally delivered by the baker who brought his mobile shop home, in an aluminium trunk carried precariously on his bicycle.

Wally and Shahnaz, knowing Malika's weakness for hygiene, would run to the table and just touch all the cakes – and that would be the beginning of the crisis. Malika refused to eat anything that had been touched by her 'unclean' siblings, leaving the two free to devour the feast.

While Malika was religious by nature, Shahnaz and Wally

were easy-going about matters of divinity. Every evening when the Maulana Sahib came to teach them their religious texts, they would insist on playing badminton with him instead. Their matches remained a closely guarded secret until Justice Beg returned home early from work one day and was shocked to see the normally solemn Maulana chasing a vigorous blow with his racquet, dressed in his loose white pyjamas and sherwani.

Despite being suitably chastised for their behaviour, Wally and his younger sister remained a conspiring pair determined to have a great childhood, until he moved to Sherwood in Nainital to complete his last two years at school.

Wally was a popular boy at school, very athletic and gregarious. His rivalry with his tall lanky classmate, the son of a well-known poet from Allahabad, was legendary. Amitabh Bachchan and he were the two most-good-looking boys in school. Understandably, the attention of the girls in the neighbouring All-Saints was divided between them. However, life mimicked the movies and they both found themselves completely smitten with the same young girl, a certain Miss Lyall. A fist-fight seemed to be the only way to settle matters and put an end to the fierce rivalry. Wally, being the boxing champion of the school, managed to defeat his opponent. Little did he know that one day Amitabh would set the screen on fire as the angry young man of Indian cinema, while Wally would watch him in awe, from his seat in a darkened hall.

When the courts closed for the long summer break the otherwise busy Justice Beg looked forward to bonding with his family in cooler weather. The Begs often spent their summers in Kashmir but the family vacation my mother remembers most vividly was when on their way to Srinagar one year they stopped in Delhi for a day to visit a very special person.

Tall iron gates swung open and their car drove past a carefully tended garden where only roses bloomed. The family was led into an elegant lounge where they waited to meet the first Prime Minister of the country.

Jawaharlal Nehru was a charming and thoughtful host. On hearing that the family was on its way to Kashmir, he said, 'I am also going to Kashmir tomorrow morning. Please do accompany me on my aircraft.' The children were excited at the thought of flying with the nation's hero and after some hesitation Justice Beg accepted the invitation.

So, early on a bright New Delhi morning, the Begs joined the Prime Minister on his flight. En route, Nehru spoke of the days of the freedom movement, when his father had taken refuge at Samiullah Beg's house in Hyderabad; the bond of friendship shared between their fathers had not been forgotten. As they flew over the Qutub Minar he pointed it out to Shahnaz. 'Do you see that?' he asked, flashing a warm smile. 'That is the famous Qutub Minar.'

My mother saw it but as she recalls, she was more entranced by the dew-fresh red rose in the Prime Minister's coat lapel and the Nehruvian aura.

The Girl with Beautiful Eyes

Sitting in my penthouse apartment today and looking back at her life, it is hard for me to imagine my mum, all of fourteen, a student of St. Mary's convent, Allahabad, with beautiful warm eyes and brown hair, carefree and oblivious of the future planned out for her. The extent of her ambition was limited to acting as the queen in the school play.

The particular day that I want to take you back to was a turning point in her life in many ways. The school bell rang as usual and it was time to go home. Like flocks of birds flying to freedom, hundreds of girls ran out of the corridors of St. Mary's to their waiting cars and parents.

Quite coincidentally, a handsome young man had accompanied his friend to pick up the friend's sister from St. Mary's. As he waited patiently, his vision blurred by the uniformed crowd of girls bursting out of the gates, he noticed a presence that was sheer energy. A beautiful young girl with sunshine in her eyes and an irresistible luminosity caught his attention.

His eyes followed her through the throng of schoolgirls as she was bundled into a waiting car veiled with curtains on all sides to keep the world from catching a glimpse of her.

The young man watched the car drive away with his muse. He was Nasir Husain, the son of the income tax commissioner of Kanpur. All of twenty-four and extremely handsome, Nasir had been struck by Shahnaz's enigmatic presence that shone through even at the age of fourteen, surrounded as she was by a swarm of uniformed young girls.

The next day, the tall young man was waiting silently once again at the gates of St. Mary's with his friend, his eyes searching for the girl who had entranced him. As the floodgates opened and waves of schoolgirls emerged from St. Mary's, he saw her appear like a flash in the afternoon sunlight and then, just as quickly, disappear into the waiting car.

For the next few days he accompanied his friend Ishrat to pick up his sister. Each time he would just stand and look at the girl with the beautiful brown curls and stunning eyes emerge and in an instant be surrounded by her chaperone, an alert-looking maid, who would lead her protectively to the waiting car. He had no idea who she was – she could be anybody; of any faith. He could sense though, that she was from a conservative family, because her car windows were concealed with curtains on all sides, a thick navy blue fabric divided the driver's seat from the back, blocking the view.

Ishrat was getting a little confused about his friend's keenness to accompany him to his sister's school every day and it seemed that it was time to confide in him.

'There is a beautiful girl, Ishrat,' said Nasir finally, 'who comes out of the school and before I can catch a glimpse of her she drives away in her car.'

'So we will need to find out who she is,' smiled Ishrat, the secret behind his friend's persistent visits to St. Marys revealed.

That afternoon they reached the gates of St. Mary's early

and stood chatting with the driver, who was steely and uncommunicative. However the nanny, Nooran, was a friendly lady; bored of waiting for her ward she was quite ready to start a conversation with the young men.

'My baby is Beg Sahab's daughter. The *bara* Judge Sahab of the high court.' She then launched into a long monologue: 'Very naughty girl, my Shahnaz baby, I know how much trouble she gives me. Every day she pulls apart the curtains of the car and peeps out and every day Memsahib shouts at me. The older baby is a very good girl but misses a lot of school.'

The young man was listening intently catching every little detail. The vigilant driver was quick to notice that Nooran was busy divulging information about the girls and he called out to the effusive lady but by now some of the mystery surrounding her identity had been solved. She was Shahnaz Beg, Justice Beg's younger daughter.

A few days later, a large white envelope was delivered with the mail to Justice Beg's residence and went into the pile of letters that sat neatly on his table waiting to be read. He went through each one of them methodically until the envelope marked 'Private' caught his eye. He studied it for a moment, then carefully slit it open with a paper knife and began reading the contents. As he read on his eyebrows shot up in surprise; his 'Chhoti Baby', as he called her, had received a marriage proposal.

In his letter, Syed Bashir Husain, the income tax commissioner of Kanpur, had eloquently described his son Nasir and proposed a union between Justice Beg's younger daughter and his son.

Amused, Nasirullah Beg walked out to where his wife sat on the patio. 'Look at this, Bibi, a marriage proposal for Shahnaz.' He laughed out loud, shaking his head. 'This is very inappropriate; do they have any idea how young she is?' he remarked dismissively.

Sayeeda Begum, however, did not share his mirth. 'She is not as young as you think,' she told her husband. 'In Hyderabad, we used to get proposals at an even younger age. How old was I when you married me?' she asked.

Justice Beg smiled guiltily. 'You were sixteen, Bibi, but that was a long time ago. Times have changed.'

'Not for me,' his wife said, taking the letter from his hands. She read it carefully and smiled. 'You should get used to the idea of our Chhoti Baby getting wedding proposals. She must get married one day, after all.'

That night Justice Beg sat down at his rich mahogany writing table and in the glow of a green spot lamp, wrote back to Mr Bashir Husain thanking him for the proposal and politely declining his offer since his daughter was far too young to marry.

Over the next few months several letters were exchanged between the men, until it was clear that the young Nasir was so much in love with Shahnaz that he was not willing to give up. In one of his letters Mr Husain offered to come down from Kanpur with his family to Allahabad to meet the Begs. Though Justice Beg did not want to let matters go any further, his wife was in favour of extending an invitation to the Husains.

'Perhaps he will be suitable for Malika,' she reasoned.

So on an icy winter afternoon, the tall handsome young man who had waited patiently on many afternoons outside St. Mary's to catch a glimpse of the girl with sparkling brown eyes, travelled with his father and elder sister from Kanpur to Allahabad. The journey between the two towns took a few hours. As he drove through the cold countryside his crisp blue suit was brushed by a film of dust that flew in through the window. In his mind he silently prepared for the most important meeting of his life, rehearsing the lines that came to his poetically inclined, deeply smitten mind.

At their home in Allahabad, Sayeeda Begum was busy preparing for the arrival of her special guests and instructing her staff to make sure there were no slip-ups. The living room had been immaculately cleaned and looked perfectly dressed to receive visitors; a bunch of multicoloured flowers had been freshly hand-picked by the mali from the garden, making a pretty centrepiece.

Unaware of the feelings she had inspired in Nasir, Shahnaz remained completely oblivious to the events that would change the course of her life. The girls rarely cared about visitors because it was a family rule that they never appeared before guests unless specially invited to.

Justice Beg sat in a corner of the veranda with his eyes buried in a book; the only refuge he could find from what he thought was a pointless exercise. He disapproved of engaging in any premature discussion on his teenage daughter's marriage and was wondering how he had allowed matters to go from declining the proposal to receiving her prospective in-laws at his home. He was concerned about his daughter's education and was extremely particular that her mind not be allowed to waver from her academic pursuits. The only reason he was meeting the Husain family was to placate his wife, who felt that, if he had his way, Shahnaz and Malika would remain unmarried for the rest of their lives. He found the excitement in the house quite bothersome and was looking forward to seeing it all over.

The olive-green Humber Snipe rolled down the driveway and ground to a halt. When the doors were opened by the staff, a dignified gentleman with a flowing beard stepped out. His eyes were dark and very intense and he had the look of quick-wittedness and intelligence that was displayed in his letters. He was followed by a lady in a chiffon sari with a moon-shaped face and a pleasant smile and a tall young man with perfectly chiselled features and a distinctly soft expression.

Mohammad Ali, Justice Beg's peon, dressed in his uniformed finery and his hallmark red-and-white turban, received the guests and ushered them into the living room where Justice Beg and his wife waited, along with their son, Waliullah. The families greeted each other and exchanged pleasantries. Mr Bashir Husain introduced the lady as his elder daughter Naseem and then turned to the young man behind him.

'This is my son, Nasir,' he said. 'You must have noticed, Beg Sahab, that he shares your name. Indeed, a good sign.'

Nasir wished them respectfully with the traditional salaam. The red tie he had chosen to wear with his light blue suit gave him a boyish freshness that accentuated his good looks. Justice Beg and Sayeeda were impressed by his grace and elegance, rare in men of his age. His politeness and genteel manner quickly won Nasir favour with the Begs. As they sat down, a huge basket of sweets was carried in as a sign of things to come.

'Beg Sahib, last night I had a most unusual dream,' started Mr Husain, 'I dreamt that my son Nasir had married your daughter.'

Justice Beg did not know how to react to this startling statement but he soon realized that Mr Husain was an engaging conversationalist and for a man who had spent his life dealing with law books and legal tangles it was fascinating to converse with such an interesting person.

My paternal grandfather was a poet, highly intelligent, with a crisp mind and a formidable presence. As he regaled the Begs with the history of his family, his son smiled on indulgently. The staff was gearing up to serve lunch and when the table was laid Mrs Beg invited her guests to move to the dining room.

Over a spread of biryani and kebabs Mr Beg tried to ask some searching questions, to quiz the young man: 'How do you like your job?'...'Which college did you go to?'... 'Economics? Good choice. They say in the sixties people will make a lot of money. Right direction'... 'Did you say tennis? I played a lot of tennis at Cambridge but not any more.'

Mrs Beg was looking on at Nasir in sheer admiration. It was clear that by now the young man had won her over. It was not just the content of the answers but the tone and the respectfulness, the unqualified politeness of the voice that stood out. A highly cultured young man emerged, someone who was brought up in the best traditions.

When lunch ended, the guests were invited to return to the living room. As the elders led the way, Nasir stepped out with Waliullah. The two stood in the veranda, chatting, but Nasir's thoughts were elsewhere. His eyes searched for Shahnaz, whom he hadn't spotted yet when she appeared suddenly like a wish come true. Dressed in a tunic and blouse, her curly brown hair in disarray, a bunch of marbles in her fist, she was headed to the garden to play her favourite game.

She stopped short, taken aback at the sight of the tall handsome man standing in the veranda and looking at her. He was unlike her father's usual guests – mostly staid members of the judicial fraternity. Nasir smiled at her, hoping she would respond but she remained still, a little stunned and awkward. Her hand opened and her fistful of marbles spilled on to the concrete floor, the sound of glass hitting cement creating an accidental symphony.

'Shahnaz,' Sayeeda Begum stood behind the young men. 'Go inside, please.'

Startled, Wally took the cue from his mother's reaction and quickly led the guest into the living room. Nasir remained distracted for the rest of the visit, his eyes moving to the door to see if he could catch another glimpse but Shahnaz was gone, hidden away in some part of the house.

When the guests rose to leave, the Begs walked them to the car to bid goodbye. 'I hope this visit is the beginning of a long relationship,' said Mr Husain.

Justice Beg smiled warmly as they shook hands but did not say anything.

Mrs Beg was extremely upset by what she felt was her daughter's indiscretion. 'Why did you have to come running into the veranda when you had been told that guests were coming?' she demanded. 'You have no shame; you are totally out of control. I think it really is time we should get you married.'

'To whom?' asked Shahnaz, tilting her head curiously.

'To the young man who came today. You ran out and took a good look at him, didn't you? He wants to marry you.'

'Marry me?' she asked surprised.

'Yes, marry you. He has no idea what an unruly girl you are.'

Her mother's reprimands faded into the background as Shahnaz's thoughts returned to the handsome man who had suddenly appeared in the veranda of her home. She smiled at the unfamiliar feeling that overcame her, one that she could not define.

That evening, Justice Beg and his wife sat down for their ritual cup of tea and discussed the events of the day and their special visitors. It was clear that Nasir's personality and demeanour had impressed Justice Beg, so much so that he had begun to regret that Shahnaz was not ready for marriage at this point.

'The boy is so handsome but of course Shahnaz is too young. Did you notice the way he bent down when he met us? And what a strange coincidence that he and I share the same name. Such a polite boy, cultured, well-educated, but I simply cannot let Shahnaz leave school to get married at fourteen.'

'Malika is not too young, she is turning eighteen this year,' said Sayeeda Begum. 'As I said before, she will be perfect for him. The Husains seem deeply religious and Malika says her namaz five times a day and is very pious. Besides, she is not keen on studying further, so we should start thinking of settling her down. Why don't you write to them and see how they feel?'

Justice Beg sat at his table once again and wrote to Mr Husain. He started by saying that he and his wife were won over by his charming son but Shahnaz was only fourteen and in no way ready for marriage. However, he added, their elder daughter Malika may be more suitable.

A few days later, Mr Husain's reply arrived on Justice Beg's table. Politely and elegantly, as was his style, Bashir Husain thanked Justice Beg for his suggestion but regretted that he was helpless in the matter. It seemed his son had given his heart to Shahnaz and was prepared to wait forever. In fact, the letter said, Nasir was so devoted to her that he had refused to meet any other girl. Leaving the matter in the hands of God, Mr Husain ended the letter saying that he would pray for his son's wish to come true some day and that he had faith in the strength of his prayers.

Although the match with Malika had not worked out, Sayeeda Begum was happy to hear that the young man was prepared to wait for Shahnaz. She had rarely, if ever, met such a personable young man and constantly kept the topic alive with her husband. But much as he liked Nasir, Justice Beg was not willing to let the matter go any further. Shahnaz was at the top of her class and a star student at St. Mary's. Her academic record was brilliant and it was clear that she had a very promising future. He was determined to give his daughter all the opportunities he had been given by his parents and when the time was right he hoped she would sit in the hallowed halls of Cambridge as he had once, with the best and the brightest in the world. He knew that even there his Shahnaz would outshine the rest.

'Let's not talk of Shahnaz's marriage again, Bibi,' he told his wife. 'After she finishes school, I am going to send her to Cambridge.'

Extremely traditional herself, Sayeeda Begum was horrified by the thought. Though she had known of her husband's plans she had never considered the possibility of them being real.

'She is not a boy,' she said softly trying to make her husband understand her feelings. 'I know you studied at Cambridge but girls in our family don't leave the house unescorted. How can you even dream of sending her to a foreign land, alone? Why don't you think of sending Wally instead? He is a boy and needs a good career.'

'So what if she is not a boy? She should get the same opportunities as one,' Justice Beg retorted. 'As for Wally, he is keen on St. Stephen's College in New Delhi and I think that will be the correct place for him.' For the man who had thrown his wife's veil away at the start of his life with her, the education of his daughter was a sacred commitment.

'Do you realize how out-of-control she will get if she lives alone? You have no idea how I manage your daughter. Ask Nooran and she will tell you. I had to buy new curtains for the car four times this month because Shahnaz tears them open to look out.'

Far from being shocked, Justice Beg seemed to approve of his daughter's actions. 'Why have you put those curtains in the car in the first place? She just wants to look out at the world,' he said with a smile.

Sayeeda Begum looked at her husband in disbelief. Marriage, she realized, was the only way to stop him from sending their daughter to study in some distant country with an alien culture.

The difference of opinion over Shahnaz's future was the couple's only point of divergence and it remained so for many years to come.

'Love is a Many-Splendored Thing'

The tiny town of Allahabad was sweltering in the heat of summer. The searing temperatures had driven everyone indoors and the normally busy streets looked desolate. Rows of rickshaw-pullers slept listlessly under the shade of the trees with few venturing out except in the late evenings. Justice Beg's home was cooled by the fragrance of wet khus which blew out of the desert cooler bringing with it a pleasant calm to rooms shielded with heavy curtains to keep the scorching sunlight away. Mango panna, rose drinks and iced coolers were sipped as antidotes to the dreaded heat and muslin kurtas with delicate chikankari became the clothes of the season.

It was the time of the year when the well-heeled families of the north left their homes for the cooler air of the mountains. Justice Beg and his family were preparing to leave for a vacation to Mussoorie. While Sayeeda Begum supervised the staff to ensure there were ample sandwiches packed for the road, the children were excitedly stuffing their bags with last-minute holiday 'essentials'.

For Shahnaz, this included her tony perm set, *the* most important piece of baggage as far as she was concerned – she had recently acquired a set to curl her already curly hair to make her look like a supermodel in a magazine – and she stashed it at the bottom of her deep canvas bag so her mother would not notice it.

Their luggage stowed away in the boot of the car, the family got into Justice Beg's beloved blue Austin and set off. Driving long distances with Justice Beg was a painful experience. The driver was not allowed to go faster than twenty-five kilometres per hour and after every twenty-five kilometres the car was stopped in the wilderness so its engine could 'rest'. The normally six-hour journey was covered in what felt like an eternity, with the Austin moving languidly in slow motion through the scorched countryside, groaning laboriously over every pothole.

When the car finally reached Mussoorie the kids clapped excitedly, glad to have finally made it to the fun spot of the summers. The turbaned doorman opened the doors of the Austin with a flourish and they spilled out, relieved to be free from the car's confines. Shahnaz, Malika and Wally stepped into the lobby of the Savoy looking exhausted but were too disciplined to complain to their father.

'The car is rested and fresh but what about my children?' Sayeeda Begum demanded of her husband, as she stepped out of the car.

The receptionist at the Savoy Hotel greeted the family with a familiar smile. 'Welcome, Justice Beg. How long will you be staying?'

'I will be staying for just two days but my family will be here for a week.'

The best mountain-facing rooms had been reserved for Justice Beg and his family. As the doors were flung open, the youngsters rushed in and fell on the beds, exhausted with the long journey.

By the evening, however, they had recovered enough to step out for an exploratory walk down the Mall, dressed in their holiday best.

In the Mussoorie of the time it was considered fashionable to take an evening stroll along the Mall, greeting other vacationing friends and acquaintances one chanced upon in the passing parade. When the youngsters were out walking, it was Wally's responsibility to watch over his sisters – a job that he enjoyed but only for a while, since this meant that he could not pursue his own interests.

At seventeen, Wally was tall and extremely handsome with aristocratic features. He was a charmer to the hilt – not surprisingly, he had a formidable female fan following.

As he walked down the Mall with his sisters by his side one evening, he spotted a group of pretty girls hanging about the mobile food-stalls that lined the sides of the street in the summers. 'Hi, Wally Beg!' They called out. He waved to them wistfully before reluctantly following his sisters. Chaperoning them was one of the more tiresome obligations of being a brother that he had to endure.

He had no trouble with Malika, who was more concerned about being home in time for her namaz. But Shahnaz more than made up for her sober sister, with her exuberance and curiosity and her penchant for disappearing into the maze of shops and by-lanes, trying to take in everything – the faux jewellery shops, the hawkers selling bright Cat-Woman-style sunglasses, the sequinned clothes, the mirrored slippers.

The Mall invariably echoed with cries of, 'Where is Shahnaz?'

'I am over here, Wally,' she would shout from some corner before disappearing again.

And then once again: 'And where is she *now*?' as Wally and Nooran exhausted themselves, searching for the unpredictable Shahnaz.

When they returned home, a distraught Nooran would pour out her complaints to Sayeeda Begum: 'Don't send me with Chhoti Baby, Begum Sahiba. I will lose her in the mountains. She does not listen to me. Send me with Malika Baby a thousand times but Chhoti Baby is not in my control.'

'She is beyond my control too,' said Wally, seizing the opportunity to be absolved of the task of chaperoning his sisters for evening walks, when all the prettiest girls from the plains were holidaying there and he could do nothing more than wave to them.

Mussoorie has a way of hiding itself away in the clouds on some days and it was on one such foggy, overcast day that the girls insisted on going for a walk on the mountain road.

'All right,' Sayeeda Begum agreed. 'But I will come along with you.'

Smartly attired in a crisp sari and walking sandals, she left the hotel with Malika by her side and Shahnaz, as always, trailing behind. Unable to blunt his conscience and desert the ladies, Wally resigned himself to another evening of chaperoning. As they took the blind turn at the end of Camel's Back Road, Sayeeda Begum stopped short in disbelief. Coming at them, almost on collision course, was Nasir in a beige suede jacket accompanied by his elder sister Naseem.

'Oh my God!' Sayeeda exclaimed. 'Wally, take the girls back immediately.'

While Wally hurriedly escorted his sisters back to the hotel, Sayeeda exchanged pleasantries with the Husains.

'What a coincidence.'

'Not really,' Naseem admitted. 'Nasir found out from Ishrat's sister that Shahnaz would be here and he dragged me all the way, hoping he would catch a glimpse of Shahnaz Bibi.'

Nasir looked away with an embarrassed grin, wishing his sister had been more subtle. Sayeeda Begum smiled indulgently at his bashfulness and shook her head. The extent of his devotion to her daughter was all too obvious and she was more convinced than ever that this gentle-natured boy was the perfect match for her daughter.

The 'chance' meeting at Camel's Back Road was a turning point in the relationship between Shahnaz and Nasir.

'Mummy, how come that boy who wants to marry me is here, too?' asked Shahnaz, when her mother returned to the hotel.

'His sister said he came here hoping to see you.'

'Really? He came all the way here to meet me?' Shahnaz sounded both flattered and confused.

Sayeeda smiled at her reaction. 'Well, I am glad your Papa has returned to Allahabad or he would have taken you back with him and put you on the first plane to England.'

'But I *want* to go to England. Papa has promised me,' her daughter replied, forgetting all about her desperate admirer.

'Shahnaz, you are a girl, not a boy. Your father doesn't understand the difference. Girls must marry and have children and build homes, not study alongside men in foreign universities. Now, if he wanted to send Waliullah I would be fine with that but unfortunately for me, you are as clever as a son should be.'

The next morning, when Mrs Beg walked into the lobby of the Savoy Hotel with Wally by her side, she found Nasir and Naseem stepping in.

'Now that we have come all the way,' said Naseem, with a polite smile, 'let's at least get to know each other. There is a very good English movie on, *Love Is a Many-Splendored Thing* and maybe we can all go and see it?' she suggested brightly.

Mrs Beg hesitated, not quite used to handling situations without her husband's advice but Wally was excited at the thought of some real entertainment finally.

'Oh, that's a movie I have been wanting to see for a while. We must see it,' he piped in, hoping to influence his mother's thought process.

'Good, then it's settled,' said Nasir. 'We will get the tickets for the afternoon show.'

Mrs Beg remained silent – this was her way of letting things move ahead in the direction she wanted.

Back in the hotel, Shahnaz was thrilled to bits at the thought of going for a movie, though she still couldn't quite believe her luck.

'What's happened to Mummy?' she asked Wally. 'Since when has she become so modern? Imagine taking us for a movie.'

Shahnaz in all her years had been allowed to see only one movie – *The King and I* – which had been recommended by her school as a must-see educational film for its students. The thought of seeing a movie in a theatre in Mussoorie was akin to going to the Moulin Rouge in Paris. Very exciting and scandalous!

Many outfits were pulled out from the cupboard, ironed, worn and then rejected; the tony perm set was heated to add bounce to her hair, while her older, more staid sister watched disapprovingly: 'She is going on as if she is the heroine of the movie,' Malika remarked.

Sayeeda Begum called out to the girls to remind them that it was time to leave. When the family stepped into the lobby they found Nasir and his sister waiting for them. The group crossed the road to watch William Holden and Jennifer Jones in one of the great romantic movies of its times in a tiny theatre in Mussoorie.

While the black-and-white images flashed on the screen, Nasir kept glancing at the beautiful girl who had him spellbound. Dressed like a lady today, she looked prettier than ever. The projector's luminous beam transporting the images created a surreal glow in which tiny insects that crossed its path lit up for an instant, like fireflies. The hissing of the spools churned in the background as the voice of Engelbert Humperdinck floated through the small theatre, singing 'Enchanted':

'Love is a many-splendored thing,
It's the April rose that only grows
In the early spring,
Love is Nature's way of giving a reason to be living,
Yes, true love's a many-splendored thing.'

A few days later, the dust-covered car made its way back down the winding hills of Mussoorie with Sayeeda Begum and her children. Shahnaz was humming the theme song from the movie she had watched and her mother had to remind her that good girls didn't hum in public. But Shahnaz was in a different world. She was gazing out of the window, reliving every moment of that afternoon she had spent in the company of the handsome man.

Justice Beg was pleased to have his family back but as the days passed he noticed that Shahnaz had started keeping to herself more than usual.

'What is the matter with her?' he asked his wife. 'Is she unwell?'

'I wanted to tell you earlier. Nasir and his family were in Mussoorie as well and they invited us for a movie. The children were very keen so I made an exception and took them. She has been very quiet since that day; I think she is thinking of him.'

Justice Beg was shocked but remained silent and thoughtful.

He was getting the distinct feeling that matters were slipping out of his control. Shahnaz continued to be quiet and withdrawn and it was obvious that what she felt was more than a passing crush. Not even Wally, her brother and best friend, could get across to her. His constant efforts – 'Shaina, come on, let's play ninepins,' or 'Shaina, a game of badminton?' – elicited nothing but silence.

Finally, Justice Beg asked his wife to speak to Shahnaz. Sayeeda spent several hours in her daughter's room and when she finally emerged, Justice Beg looked up anxiously at his wife.

'What did she say?' he asked.

'She would like to marry Nasir,' said Sayeeda Begum.

'But she is not old enough,' Justice Beg protested. 'Doesn't she realize she is too young for marriage?'

'I think it is best if they get engaged now and marry when she is old enough,' Sayeeda suggested.

Justice Beg was despondent; he saw his dreams of making Shahnaz the next star of the family, fading; his hopes of her studying at Cambridge dashed by a chance meeting in the hills. He tried speaking to Shahnaz directly but her traditional upbringing did not allow her to speak of marriage with her father. Justice Beg was in a terrible dilemma, one that he always maintained was the toughest in his life – being a liberal man, he could not forcibly keep his daughter from a marriage she wanted, nor could he stand by and watch Shahnaz turn her back on the bright future he foresaw for her.

Ultimately, the decision was Shahnaz's and so it was with a heavy heart that he told his wife to speak to the Husains about a token exchange of rings.

Shahnaz Beg was engaged at the age of fourteen, her only ambition to be the wife of the most handsome man she had ever laid her eyes upon.

A Love as Young as Innocence

My mother remembers the biggest advantage of being engaged: 'Imagine, for the two years of my engagement I didn't need to do my homework,' she smiles, looking back on the early days of love. 'He came down every weekend and went through my pile of books and did all my math sums for me.'

When Nasir visited the Beg home he was strategically given the remotest room on the top floor, from where he would look down and watch the night-time ritual of the Beg household in the summers. The family had a tradition of sleeping in the back veranda of the house, since Justice Beg believed in the benefits of eight hours of pure oxygen. Five beds with mosquito nets were put in a row and table fans were placed to ensure a pleasant flow of breeze through the night. Water jugs shielded with muslin covers and glasses were placed on tall stools beside each bed.

One night Nasir looked on wistfully at the white tent-like units and decided that he was going to try and wake up Shahnaz. He took a glass of water and aimed it straight on Shahnaz's mosquito net before carefully pouring it down.

'*Allah!*' came a shrill voice from the white enclosure and Sayeeda Begum jumped out of her bed looking stunned and wet. Nasir was quick to realize that he had mistakenly drenched his mother-in-law-to-be and moved away in a flash.

'Where did this water come from?' said Justice Beg, confused. The whole family was out of their beds and then they all looked up. Shahnaz smiled gently at the clear night sky.

The weekends were always exciting for Shahnaz and as the months passed Nasir watched, fascinated, as she sat with her pile of books, reading through her lessons, until one day, reams of homework later, he found himself helping her with her final exams at school. Shahnaz walked out of St. Mary's, a high school graduate with no ambitions of glory other than becoming Shahnaz Husain.

Two years into the engagement, Nasir pressed the family for an early wedding. Sayeeda Begum, who had found the long engagement very stressful and was on tenterhooks ensuring that the couple did not break any family traditions, agreed readily and after some discussion between the two families it was decided that Shahnaz would wed Nasir Husain on the twenty-fifth of December.

With Shahnaz's wedding date fixed, Sayeeda Begum plunged herself into the arrangements of the wedding. One of the plans on the pre-wedding agenda was a trip to Hyderabad, to seek Amina's blessings and to complete the trousseau with traditional clothes and jewellery. The flight to Hyderabad was bumpy and long with two stopovers en route. Shahnaz looked out into the clouds and waited excitedly for her grandmother's loving embrace.

When the tall gates of Rahat Manzil were opened, Sayeeda Begum smiled wistfully. She looked around at the manicured lawns and wondered if Shahnaz could ever imagine the lifestyle that she had once experienced here.

Amina was delighted to see Sayeeda and her younger daughter and the next week was spent in bonding with the family. Rahat Manzil now had Amina along with her sons and their wives and children living there, ensuring that there was never a dull moment.

It was the month of Ramzan so the family woke up to an early morning Sehri. After a day of starvation they would feast together in the evenings with friends and visitors who had dropped in; the environment at Rahat Manzil remained simultaneously festive and pious through the holy month.

One morning, when Amina opened the dark and damp store-room where the foodgrain for the family was stocked, she felt a sudden jab in her foot – as though a spanner had caught it. She looked down and shuddered at the sight of a huge scorpion. Backing out of the store she returned to her room, her foot bleeding and lay down on her bed. The first to notice her state was one of her grandsons and in an instant the entire family was by her side. The family doctor was called for and after giving her some quick first-aid he sent for an anti-venom serum to prevent the poison from affecting her vital organs.

As he filled the liquid in the syringe Amina looked at the doctor intently and then slowly shook her head.

Confused, he asked her, 'Madam is there a problem?'

Her speech was halting but clear: 'It is Ramzan and I have not broken a roza for forty years. I will not let you give me the injection and break my faith at this age.' The doctor looked shocked; her sons, daughters and the children standing around her looked anxious.

'Begum Sahiba, I am a Muslim also, trust me, this injection is to save your life, you must not refuse it.'

Amina looked stoic and firm. She shook her head even as her family appealed to her to give in. Finally they relented, respecting her wishes and her unflinching faith. Then, making a protective ring, they sat around her and prayed to the God she was devoted to. Shahnaz's eyes brimmed with tears as she watched her grandmother's face turning paler by the moment.

The clock ticked on and with every breath Amina felt an acute internal pain. The hands of the clock moved slower than the poison flowing through her body and as the sun turned into an orange ball of fire, the humming of prayers grew into a frenzied crescendo with the belief that she had almost made it. But then an indigo hue rose from behind her silver hair shadowing her face and with a soft 'Allah' Amina faded away.

The visit to Hyderabad left Shahnaz and Sayeeda saddened beyond belief. What had been planned as a family reunion had turned into a tragic event. Shahnaz remained silent on the flight back remembering each magnified moment of her grandmother's journey to a world beyond; a memory that would stay with her for years to come. She looked out at the clouds; they now had a different meaning for her.

The family had suffered a tragedy and the grief persisted, until Sayeeda, every bit her mother's daughter, made a conscious effort to dispel the gloom and return to the task of her daughter's marriage arrangements. It was essential for her to encase her grief within and end the days of mourning so that the wedding festivities could begin with happiness.

Shahnaz was turning sixteen on the fifth of November and this was to be a special birthday. She was engaged to be married and had dreamy expectations from her fiancé.

'So what's he doing for your birthday?' asked her friends with a hint of excitement and girlish envy. She had invited them over for brunch. Since their insistence on meeting her handsome fiancé was getting to be too much to handle, she had asked her mother if Nasir could make an appearance.

With just a month to go for the wedding, Sayeeda Begum relented grudgingly: 'Don't let him stay too long; five minutes or so is fine.'

Nasir arrived the day before Shahnaz's birthday, a small ring tucked away in his bag. The gold ring had two hands with ruby cuffs sliding to enclose a heart in the centre. On the heart was inscribed the word 'Cuckoo', his endearment for her in the early days of their relationship. As a child, I often held the ring in my hand with fascination, admiring the perfect symbol of my parents' love and bonding. It remains my mother's most treasured possession today.

That night, while the family slept, Nasir slipped out into the garden where he was joined by a few obliging staff members who were happy to find some excitement in the Judge's solemn home. With the help of his eager team he spent the next several hours creating the surprise he had planned for Shahnaz's birthday – a canopy of little multicoloured flags over the garden. Reds, blues, greens, yellows sparkled in the glistening moonlight. When he finally stood back and looked at the decorations, a smile of satisfaction lit his face. He couldn't wait for morning, for Shahnaz to wake up and see the result of his love's labour – the brilliant display of colour.

Shahnaz was up early the next day, eager not to miss even a moment of her birthday.

'I have a surprise for you,' said Nasir leading her into the garden. She looked up and like the child that she was, she began to cry. Nasir was shocked; the dew had drenched the paper decorations; the colours had run, leaving them faded and pathetic.

'Oh my God, what happened?' he said.

His team of volunteers stood around looking helpless.

'Baba, it was very moist and cold last night and the thin paper flags got completely wet.'

'What will my friends say? They will laugh at me,' Shahnaz cried, knowing that a bunch of expectant and curious girls was going to arrive soon.

'Let me try and redo it,' offered a harassed Nasir.

'There is no time. I will just have to face the embarrassment.'

Nasir was miserable and disappointed. The shops were closed and there was nothing he could do to save the situation.

'I think it is best to remove the decorations,' Sayeeda Begum suggested in an attempt to mend matters. But Shahnaz had no such plans.

'No, Mummy, please let them be. At least I will be able to tell my friends that he did this for me even if it got ruined.'

A few hours later Shahnaz's friends arrived, dressed in their best salwar-kameezes, their hair done up in the styles of the time – tight braids, fringes and soft curls – excited at the prospect of meeting their friend's fiancé.

The girls walked in and looked up, confused. Staring doubtfully at the wilted pieces of paper, they asked, 'What happened?'

'He climbed the ladder and put them up himself,' said Shahnaz, pointing proudly to the remnants of her fiancé's work of art. 'He just didn't realize how cold Allahabad is and that the dew would drench them.'

'Oh, poor you, Shahnaz,' her friends commiserated.

'No, don't say poor me. After all, what matters is that he did this *just* for me. See all those long strings? He was awake all night tying each one himself.'

The look of envy was back on her friends' faces. After all, Shahnaz was the only one amongst them who had experienced real love at an age when most of them were not even aware of what its molecules were. Nasir was a little embarrassed at the thought of being inspected by a bunch of schoolgirls but Shahnaz had made him promise that he would meet her friends. The chatter died as soon as he walked into the garden. Everyone froze in awkward shyness.

'Hello, I am Nasir,' he said, a little confounded by the sudden silence that had fallen over the crowd. The girls stared at him as though he was an alien. Mumbling a polite 'enjoy yourselves', he made a hasty retreat.

'Oh my *God!* Shahnaz, you lucky girl! He is *so* handsome. Now we know why you gave up your studies to get married.'

Shahnaz beamed like a queen bee as she stood in the middle of the garden, enjoying the limelight while Engelbert crooned her favourite tune of love on a small gramophone.

'By the way, did anyone notice,' she said, twirling the gold ring on her finger. 'He looks *just* like Tony Curtis?'

The Brocade Bride

At sixteen, my mother made a beautiful bride. She wore the traditional bridal dress of Muslims – a red gharara in silk with intricate zardozi patterns dreamed up by an artisan for the wedding of a girl destined one day to be queen. It is said that when a wedding dress is made, the weavers and embroiderers say a prayer over it and anoint it with their love and sweat. So it must have been, for Shahnaz stepped into a life that unfolded in strange and intricate ways, in a manner not unlike the patterns on her dress. On her forehead, she wore her grandmother's 'tika' like a blessing – a family heirloom that, years later, I wore on my wedding day too.

Moti Mahal, the marriage venue, was adorned with lights and strings of mogras and roses, their mild fragrance mingling with the rising aroma of the biryani being prepared. The melodious notes of the shehnai wove their way through the house to where my mother sat, reminding her that she would leave her parents' home that night. Her heart pounded with anxiety and a touch of excitement. Malika, who had been married six months earlier, sat by her younger sister, wearing a golden gharara, whispering sisterly advice in her ear.

In a Muslim wedding the bride remains in a private area where only women are allowed but it is tradition to bring her to the window to see her baraat approach. As the beating of the drums grew louder and the marriage procession drew closer, my mother's friends and cousins came to her and led her to the window. She peered through the drapes to take in the lights and the magic of her wedding night in all its magnificence. She gazed out in awe and suddenly she began to feel very important: 'Is all this for me?' she wondered happily.

She waited by the window to catch a glimpse of her Prince Charming, watching patiently as first a row of horses appeared, followed by a row of elephants and camels. It reminded her of being at the circus, which was probably the most spectacular event she had ever seen. Finally, she spotted her bridegroom in a convertible car, wearing a gold brocade sherwani, his handsome face hidden behind a cascade of flowers. As he lifted the sehra away from his face, silence fell over the night and the sounds and lights faded; all Shahnaz could see was the face of the man she was going to be with for the rest of her life.

She spotted her father, towering over the crowd in a sleek black sherwani, his full six-foot-three-inch frame held upright as he strode forward with Wally and Malika's husband Azhar by his side and welcomed the immediate family members in the baraat – a formidable party of eight brothers and sisters led by my paternal grandfather.

As the baraat settled down, everyone's eye was on the watch since it was decided that the nikah would take place before sunset, before the *Maghrib ki Namaz*, or the evening prayers.

The bride was placed like a sacred object of infinite beauty on a maroon velvet cladding embellished with rich gold embroidery with huge bolsters on either side. It was the cover that her mother had sat on for her nikah and on which I sat for mine, making it another wedding heirloom.

Just then there was a loud knock on the door and instantly my mother's face was covered with a red bridal veil; she sat concealed and secure inside it, as though it were a private chamber where she could hide away. The knocking grew louder and when one of the girls opened the door, they were taken aback to see Justice Beg stride in. His face looked flushed and grim. The room fell silent, the giggling and mirth fading away as they realized that this was not in the normal course of things.

Looking straight ahead at where his daughter sat, he requested that he be left alone with the bride. The air was heavy with tension as Shahnaz uncovered her face to look at her father.

'Baby,' he said softly. 'Listen to me carefully. The bridegroom's family had promised me that a special document giving equal rights of divorce would be signed but at the last moment they have backed out. You know the principles I have lived by. I cannot let you marry under such circumstances. I am sending them back; this marriage will not take place.'

The starry-eyed bride stared at her father in confusion, the unreal situation playing itself like a dream going suddenly and inexplicably wrong.

Sayeeda Begum walked into the room, looking anxious and harried. 'What are you doing?' she asked. 'Do you really think that it is wise for you to send the baraat back? Will anyone marry Shahnaz after that and who will explain to the whole world why the boy left?'

Sayeeda Begum, a traditional woman who had made peace with her Cambridge-educated husband's liberal ways, was distraught at the prospect of the wedding, which was now in full swing, being wrapped up abruptly and the guests sent home while her young daughter sat, dressed in her bridal finery, the auspicious tika of her grandmother already on her forehead.

'Shahnaz,' she said softly yet firmly, ignoring her husband. 'The Maulvi is coming in for your nikah, please give your approval for the wedding.'

'Shahnaz,' said Justice Beg as he turned to leave the room. 'You know how I feel. I am against this marriage.'

Justice Beg felt strongly against the ceremony going ahead without the commitment made to him being met and his protective fatherly instincts made him want to rescue his daughter from the bondage of a virtual child marriage at the last hour. He was hoping against hope that Shahnaz would decline the nikah and that he could fly her down to England to pursue her studies in the corridors of learning where he had spent his youth. There were repeated knocks at the door. It was Meher Apa.

'Where are you, Baji? It is just twenty minutes for *Maghrib* and the girl's nikah must start immediately.'

Justice Beg and his wife stepped out into the sea of humanity that had built up outside.

'*Mubarak ho, Beg Sahab, tahedil se aaj ka din aapko mubarak ho.*'

Justice Beg, flushed and red-faced, went through the motions of social niceties; politely acknowledging the surreal montage of faces and people. Sayeeda Begum, her head covered, greeted her guests graciously, the tension of what may happen barely showing on her face. On a podium dressed with flowers and lights sat the bridegroom with his family and his closest friend Ishrat by his side. The mikes were adjusted so that everyone present could hear the nikah. The music was turned off and a short customary announcement was made to let all present know that the nikah was about to start. Silence fell over the festivities and suddenly this was not just a party – it was a sacred occasion that would bond two lives together forever.

Sayeeda Begum took the lead and requested the Maulana to move to the girl's chamber with the assigned witnesses. A small group of close family and friends proceeded to where the bride waited, her head weighed down by the heavy veil. The Maulana sat near the bride along with two male witnesses who were to verify that they had heard the acceptance of the bride. With the mikes adjusted, the sounds of my mother's private cocoon within the chiffon chamber were now exposed to the world at large as the guests outside waited anxiously to hear the girl's acceptance.

'Bibi Shahnaz Beg, daughter of Mirza Nasirullah Beg, do you accept your nikah with Syed Nasir Husain son of Syed Bashir Husain with a meher of five thousand rupees?'

The question was answered with silence.

'She is shy,' whispered Meher Apa nervously.

The Maulana repeated the question and once again there was complete silence. The tension in the air was palpable.

'I am asking you now for the third and last time. Bibi Shahnaz Beg, daughter of Mirza Nasirullah Beg, do you accept your nikah with Syed Nasir Husain, son of Syed Bashir Husain?'

My mother was sobbing by now, her father's voice echoed in her head. *'Remember, Shahnaz, I am against this marriage.'* He was the man she worshipped and he could do her no wrong. She trusted him and then she remembered her mother's eyes that had appealed to the woman in her.

'Shahnaz, say yes to the nikah,' whispered Meher Apa.

Justice Beg looked tense; his wife, her hand on her daughter's shoulder, was turning pale.

Overwhelmed by the energies that were working around her, the lump that had formed in her throat burst into an audible sob. The air echoed with, '*Haan ho gayee! Mubarak ho, dulhan ne haan kar dee.*'

The group then moved out to where the boy sat with his family. In a crisp and clear voice the Maulana asked, 'Do you, Syed Nasir Husain, son of Syed Bashir Husain, accept Bibi Shahnaz Beg, daughter of Mirza Nasirullah Beg, as your wife, with a meher of five thousand rupees?'

My father said, '*Qabool hai.*'

The question was repeated twice more and each time the contract of marriage was affirmed with '*Qabool hai.*'

The words echoed through the ancient columns of Moti Mahal and reached the room where Shahnaz sat, her head swirling in confusion. As is customary, the family members embraced their closest and the air rung with sounds of '*Mubarak*' in a chorus of different voices.

My parents were married.

My mother was now Shahnaz Husain.

The air in Moti Mahal blew easy once more; the music was turned on again restoring the atmosphere of gaiety and celebration. The cooks were given the clarion call and with the gusto that comes to culinary masters before serving a feast, they set about lighting the coal fires and churning the giant handis. The iron rods on which the kebabs were to be skewered were heated over the fires so the meat would cook inside-out. Long tables were lined with chairs for the guests to sit and enjoy the food rather than struggle with balancing laden plates. Lucknowis believe that you must first sit in comfort, take a deep breath and then unhurriedly relish each morsel of your meal to the accompaniment of some light conversation, perhaps a *sher* from Ghalib and in doing so compliment the chef properly for his efforts.

A special table was set for the groom's family; Wally and his brother-in-law Azhar supervised the arrangements for the baraatis personally. My father, finally relieved of his heavy sehra, sat with his family, beaming with happiness.

Justice Beg and his wife sat red-eyed and silent, facing the impending departure of their daughter. As the last course of shahi tukra was served, the festivities came to an end and the wedding guests prepared to leave.

Inside the house, my mother sat silently. Her plate of food had been returned untouched. Her mind was in a swirl; what should have been the happiest moment of her life had turned into a disjointed chain of chaotic events. Yet, as the realization and seriousness of what had happened sank in, she felt a numbing calm, as though a dreaded storm had passed. She could already feel the pull of the invisible, sacred ties that bond her with her husband forever, as she got ready to set out on a new journey.

Meher Apa, my mother's guardian angel, removed her bridal headgear to rest her shoulders for a while and gently wiped her eyes with wet cotton before touching up her make-up in a vain attempt to rekindle her girlish brightness.

The podium for the '*arsimusuf*' – the traditional ceremony when the couple see each other's faces for the first time – was ready. The bridegroom's sisters and family accompanied him inside to the podium and sat around him, smiling and laughing. My mother was led into the room by her sister and family and was made to sit facing her husband. A red chiffon dupatta was flung over their heads and a mirror was slipped between them so my father could see her reflection as a bride for the first time. It was a magical moment; her face shimmered in the glass, her eyes shut, as my father saw an image that no one else would ever see.

Leaving her family was very painful and my mother remembers breaking down when she hugged her father, feeling as though she had betrayed him in some way. Her husband gently put his arm around her and led her to the waiting car that drove away silently into the night while Justice Beg looked on with a heavy heart.

A Married Woman

Nasir and Shahnaz went to Mussoorie for their honeymoon where they stayed at the Savoy and walked down together in the evening to watch a movie at the tiny theatre full of memories. The henna on her hands shone in the glow of the cinema hall as she wiped her eyes, moved by the dramatically performed scenes in *Mother India*. Revisiting the movie hall in Mussoorie was a perfect beginning to their new lives.

The end of the honeymoon brought with it the sudden realization that marriage was a multi-layered and complex mosaic; not quite a dreamboat but a ship with many travellers. My mother entered her new home in Swarup Nagar in Kanpur with expectations and hopes but soon found that it wasn't the cosy love-nest she had imagined her first home would be – instead, it was a large house where an extended joint family lived together.

The Husains were a strongly patriarchal family and my grandfather, Abba, inspired fear and respect; his word, quite simply, was never questioned. He was aware of the effect he had on his family and he presided over his household with strict codes of conduct. Perhaps being the father of eight children had something to do with his authoritarian style. My grandmother, Amma, was soft-natured and caring but never opposed her husband.

My mother's early days in Kanpur were claustrophobic; she moved out of her room gingerly, afraid of being reprimanded by her father-in-law on issues that had never before crossed her mind. She became reclusive and preferred staying in her room. For a while she remained engrossed in unpacking her trousseau – the rows of boxes with neatly packed clothes that her mother had collected for her. It was a veritable treasure trove for a girl who had had an austere childhood with a relatively sparse wardrobe. She gasped at the zari saris, the pure white, pleated mermaid sari that became her favourite, the silks, the chiffons, the bags and jewellery and suddenly she developed a penchant for dressing up. She would occasionally emerge from her room, after making sure that Abba was away, walking awkwardly in her new high-heeled shoes, dressed to the hilt in the middle of the day with nowhere in particular to go.

While looking through her trousseau one day, my mother chanced upon what she remembers as a 'mousy looking' shawl. *Why did Mummy give me such an ugly shawl,* she wondered. She called for the family tailor and asked him to cut up the shawl and line one of her kurtas with it. When her mother heard of her daughter's ingenuity she was speechless for a few moments. 'Do you have any idea what that shawl *was*?' she asked. It was a priceless shahtoosh.

Though she still re-invents her wardrobe with impulsive decisions now that the rare shahtoosh is banned, my mother remembers that incident as her greatest designing faux-pas.

Once the cases of clothes were unpacked and placed neatly in the cupboards, the high-heeled shoes tried on repeatedly and returned to their racks, the jewellery admired with awe, her days as a newly-married woman began to feel monotonous; dressing up and waiting for her husband to return seemed like a depressing life for a lovely girl with boundless energy. Her two younger brothers-in-law were rarely home, the youngest sister, Yasmin, a pretty girl, was at school most of the day, while the older three sisters were married – though they dropped in often to meet their parents. The eldest brother, Mushir, was married to a very beautiful and demure girl who seemed completely at ease in her role as a submissive daughter-in-law. She always kept her face lowered in front of the elders with her head decorously covered.

My mother's effervescent personality was a stark contrast to hers and though she tried to conform to the ways of her new family the stifling environment made it difficult for her to find a sense of peace in her new home.

The evenings were spent with the family sitting down together to dinner at a long table. No one spoke much; it was a prerogative left to my grandfather. My parents sometimes went out for movies and shopping trips but would rush back because my grandfather would be sitting up, anxiously waiting for their return.

My father was very keen to see that his young wife was happy and was prepared to go to any extent to see her smile. 'I would treat your mum like a child, indulging her every whim,' he often told me. Even though he wanted to give her every possible happiness, it was clear that taking issue with his father was not an option. No one in the family ever contradicted Abba. It was a natural instinct in his presence to say, 'Ji, Abba'; an instinct that he had diligently inculcated in the family.

It had been two months since the wedding and Justice Beg was getting impatient to call upon his daughter's in-laws and remind them of their second promise. The fact that Shahnaz was just sixteen and had not completed her studies bothered him. He could no longer bring himself to sit back and watch his daughter go through life with just a school certificate. He had been assured by the Husains that Shahnaz would be allowed to join college and finish her studies after her marriage; it was the only reason he had agreed to the match.

When Justice Beg's car finally drove up the long driveway of the Swarup Nagar house, Shahnaz excitedly ran up to the door to welcome her father to her new home. He smiled when he saw her but his smile did not reach his eyes. He was still smarting from the events of the wedding and wore a determined look on his face.

My mother was looking every bit the new bride – her hair was plaited with tassels, her wrists were heavy with bangles and she wore a fair amount of jewellery even though it was a casual morning at home. It was obvious to Justice Beg that his daughter was going out of her way to be the perfect daughter-in-law.

'Enough of all this, baby,' he told her. 'Get out of this fancy dress; it's time you started pursuing your education again.'

My mother remained silent, avoiding her father's eyes but he knew instantly what was happening.

'Do you want to study further, Shahnaz?' he asked his daughter.

My mother nodded her head, silently.

'Have your in-laws refused to allow you to go back to school?'

'They have. But Tutu told me not to worry,' she said quickly, hoping to defuse the situation. 'He will educate me later. He is very supportive, Papa, but I know it's not easy for him to defy Abba.'

Justice Beg's eyes turned bloodshot with anger as he looked at his innocent daughter. 'I refuse to leave you here. You are leaving with me this instant,' he roared.

The tussle between her father's dreams for her and her role as a traditional, newly-married woman was never so strong. When

Abba entered the room the tension in the air was palpable. The conflict between my grandfathers was never so pronounced; it was a 'clash of cultures'. Two strong-willed men stood on either side of a chasm – one a Cambridge-educated liberal, a believer in the oneness of all religions, the other a senior bureaucrat, a devout practising Muslim who said his namaz five times a day; one who championed equal opportunity for women despite the constraints of tradition, the other whose beliefs told him that a woman's place was in the home and within its boundaries.

There was no right or wrong here, just deep differences in culture. My mother was at the centre of their conflict and it was clear that neither of them would bend.

'Are you coming with me, Shahnaz and becoming an educated woman or are you going to accept this life?'

My mother knew that this time she needed to listen to her father or else she would be nothing more than an uneducated doormat all her life. While Justice Beg sat in the living room, she went in to talk to her husband.

My father tried to reason with her, he explained to her that it was his family and not he who was against her pursuing her education. He promised to enrol her into a good college as soon as he could. But Shahnaz's mind was fraught with indecision and the only thing she could do was sob on her husband's shoulder.

Justice Beg waited restlessly, hoping Shahnaz would have the courage to make the decision to leave with him. He looked at his watch impatiently and just when he was beginning to worry that she had buckled under the pressure of the moment, to his immense relief, she stepped into the room, holding a suitcase. My mother looked back at her husband and what was exchanged between them was not a goodbye but an affirmation of unwavering love, regardless of the situation.

The journey from Kanpur to Allahabad took just four hours but it felt like an eternity as the Austin made its way over the bumpy country roads, passing through villages growing dim in the fading light. With tears brimming in her eyes, my mother asked her father if it was right for her to have left her husband and come away.

'You are only sixteen, baby and the only thing that is right is that I make sure you become a well educated woman who can stand on her own feet. You have to be independent.'

Justice Beg continued his pep talk while Shahnaz gazed listlessly out through the window until the rolling motion of the car lulled her into an exhausted slumber.

She woke up a few hours later to excited screams.

'Sahab has brought Chhoti Baby home.'

The servants were all crowding around the car to greet their Chhoti Baby. Sayeeda Begum was shocked; she hugged her daughter and then led her to her old room. Mother and daughter sat silently for a long time. Finally, Sayeeda Begum broke the silence and softly asked her daughter, 'Did your father force you to leave Nasir and come home?'

'No. Papa just asked me but I decided to come home,' Shahnaz replied, feeling it was best to leave out the confrontation between her father and father-in-law.

'Don't worry yourself too much,' said Sayeeda, calling out to the maid to heat some oil. As Shahnaz sat wondering what the future held for her, she felt the familiar soothing movements of Nooran's fingers massaging hot oil into her hair.

That night, when his wife questioned the wisdom of his actions, Justice Beg adamantly maintained that he had made the correct decision.

'They refused to let her pursue her education. They let me down a second time,' he explained to his wife.

But in Sayeeda's world the husband's home was sacred and marriages were forever. Though educated at Panchgani Convent herself, she felt her husband was forsaking Shahnaz's entire future for a degree. 'Have you thought of her living her life alone?' she asked him. 'We will not be by her side forever. I know you feel betrayed but remember they are very traditional people. Maybe it's hard for them to accept this.'

'I was against the marriage from the very beginning but I gave in on two conditions. I had to accept the first condition being broken because my daughter was in her bridal dress but this issue is very vital to me. I will not allow Shahnaz to remain uneducated, especially when she wants to study further,' Justice Beg replied.

Shahnaz was confused and depressed over the next few weeks. She missed her husband every waking moment, which showed her how deeply in love with him she was. Her father kept plying her with brochures of different colleges and universities but her thoughts were somewhere else.

Her mother was always by her side, strong and supportive, reminding her that a woman's happiness was where her heart led her. It was while she was struggling with thoughts of love and betrayal, of guilt and sorrow that she found out that she was pregnant.

'Shahnaz is going to have a baby,' Sayeeda Begum told her husband.

The news that his daughter was expecting a child was the final blow to Justice Beg's plans for Shahnaz. She had become a woman before her time and he realized he had no choice other than to step back and let her make up her mind about her future.

'Papa, I love Tutu very much and all this confusion is tearing me apart,' Shahnaz confessed. 'I have decided that I will keep my married life together and I will plan out my education with my husband. I have learnt my values from Mummy and I can't break up my marriage for anything, especially now that I have to think of my baby too.'

My mother returned to a very difficult life in Kanpur. Though my father was kind and loving as always, the rest of the family, particularly Abba, had been slighted by her decision to go home with her father. Taming her into a more self-effacing daughter-in-law became a part of her re-introduction into the family.

The months that followed were stressful for my mother; her pregnancy was advancing and she felt hapless, marooned in an environment where she was left without any escape routes. The spirit of a girl with boundless energy was stifled in an atmosphere that continually reminded her of her role as a traditional daughter-in-law.

Eyebrows went up when poetic graffiti was discovered on the veranda walls – the charcoal smudges were the outpourings of a bright girl who felt as though she were slowly suffocating. My father was deeply upset when he read the jagged letters on the wall and he tried to reason with his young wife that it was only a question of time. 'When the baby comes,' he said, 'I promise you, Shunno, we will move out of Kanpur. I am trying to get a posting to Lucknow where you will have your own home. Just trust me.'

My father's deep affection for her comforted my mother and she went through her days with the faith that life would change somehow once her child was born. In the oppressive atmosphere of her new home my mother's greatest support within the family remained her mother-in-law who went out of her way to be gentle and kind to the girl who had entered her family. Amma was calm and loving, with a warm heart and affectionate eyes. My father inherited many of his finest qualities from her.

Seeing my mother looking troubled and depressed my father felt concerned about her and surprised her with a vacation to Mussoorie. Being back in the tiny hill station where they had first met was a perfect break for both of them and soon her inherent spirit was back. In the day she browsed the familiar shops for trinkets and in the evenings they went for walks on Camel's Back Road reliving many memories. As they entered the Savoy one evening she excitedly read a poster that announced the May Queen Ball.

'Oh Tutu,' she gushed, 'I am entering the contest.'

My father looked down at her baby bulge and smiled. 'You can't, you are looking too obviously pregnant.'

'I will wear a silk sari and wrap myself up,' she retorted confidently.

My father played along, not wanting to discourage her. On the day of the ball she remained on the dance floor, determined to win but sadly when the winners were announced she did not figure anywhere. She was later told that an argument had broken out between the judges and finally the ones who felt that pregnant ladies should be disqualified had prevailed.

Not winning the May Queen Ball was unacceptable to my mother; winning was ingrained in her being – it was the most vital part of her nature. She had to win, there *had* to be a way out.

The next evening, Shahnaz went to the local stationery shop on the Mall and bought chart paper, golden sheets of foil, pouches of glitter and a bottle of glue. She went back to the hotel and Nasir watched, amused, as she took a pair of scissors and cut out a tall crown, diligently stuck on the tinsel and sprinkled the glitter all over it. Holding up the shiny headgear in her hands she looked at it and smiled approvingly. Then she wore a silk sari and brushed every unruly curl into place. 'Come on, Tutu, let's go to the photographers,' she announced when she was dressed.

My father looked surprised. 'Why?' he asked.

'I want to photograph myself with the crown. You see, I did not get the May Queen title because of a technicality, so actually I *did* win.'

My father tried to digest her logic but gave up and accompanied her.

At the studio she placed the cardboard crown on her head and smiled into the camera with the confidence of a born winner – all of which makes me feel that if you perceive yourself a winner the world follows in that belief. Even when she lost, my mother continued to believe she had triumphed. She did not recognize defeat.

Losing was never a choice for Shahnaz Husain.

My mother returned to the warmth of her parents' home to deliver her child. Two weeks into her eighth month, she was playing with her pet baby goat when it slipped from her grasp and ran away. Her huge stomach notwithstanding, she instinctively chased after the animal and tripped and fell in the process. Within minutes she was bundled into a car with her mother holding onto her and her father sitting silently beside her wearing a worried look.

The hospital in Allahabad was ill-equipped to deal with emergencies but fortunately there were no complications. I, the baby who reunited my parents, was born on the twenty-seventh of November.

My father wanted to call me 'Resham' and Abba had decided on the name 'Talat'. However, my mother's decision to name me after the princess of Hyderabad stood firm and I became Nelofar Husain.

Sunshine and Green Grass

Justice Beg, with a sola topi on his head, stood at the Lucknow railway station beside his wife, waiting anxiously for their daughter and her family to arrive. His eyes kept glancing at his watch, betraying his impatience. His official entourage stood beside him. Every now and then a passerby would stop and bow respectfully before the Judge and he would nod politely back at them. Finally the ground hummed with the vibration of the approaching train. Justice Beg felt a gust of hot air hit his face as the train rolled past him, each open window a moving postcard, until it ground to a screeching halt.

'Papa,' he heard an excited voice and spotted his Chhoti Baby jumping off the train. Soon she was hugging her parents, her eyes moist with relief and happiness.

Having returned to the Lucknow courts, my grandfather was pleased to be back in his hometown, especially now that Shahnaz and her family had moved here too.

For Shahnaz and Nasir, leaving behind the austere joint family home and moving to a new city was liberating. Nasir had kept his promise to his young wife and they were finally in Lucknow to make their first home together. It was the first step towards a life that would give them a chance to fulfil their dreams and aspirations.

My mother remembers that first journey to freedom when she boarded the train to Lucknow, amidst the sounds and smells, the chaos and clamour of the Kanpur station. The cool night air blew on her face, and she felt a sense of deep calm as the train pulled away from the city where she had remained an emotional captive. Reaching Lucknow meant crossing an invisible barrier to a life where she would have the liberty to follow her bliss.

Driving through the streets of Lucknow in the old faithful navy blue Austin, Shahnaz and Nasir reached their new address at C-9, Dilkhusha. She looked out of the window and smiled, soaking in the unmistakable serenity she felt as she stared at her new home. It was obvious that the place had been not been lived in for some time. The grass was overgrown and the paint was chipped but it was heaven for Shahnaz. She had never expected paradise to come to her; she always created her own.

The small, two-storeyed house was painted in the customary not-quite-white-not-quite-yellow distinctive of Indian government homes for generations. With its wonderful front garden – which became the venue for my birthday parties over the next few years – this home would mean more to my mother than all the opulent ones that followed.

She was thrilled when she saw the empty rooms in the charming house because it meant that she would experience the joy of decorating her own space for the first time. The nineteen-year-old Mrs Husain had every intention of making her home completely out of the ordinary. Her enthusiasm and creativity were set free and she quickly ordered her first set of furniture from a store called 'Modern Homes'.

Every piece was personally designed and was lovingly nicknamed

– the violin settee, the paisley shaped dining table reminiscent of a Salvador Dali painting and the sofa set with legs shaped like deer horns. She was stamping her surroundings with the highly individual style that would become such an intrinsic part of her image in the years ahead.

The sixties was a glorious decade all over the world. It was a time when Elvis and Kennedy moved hearts and Martin Luther King exulted, 'Free at last!' A time when rebellion was legitimized and the futility of war and conflict challenged by a counter-cultural movement that spread across the globe, even touching the quaint, quiet town of Lucknow.

I have a charming memory of my mother wearing stretch pants and a short-sleeved top, learning the latest dance that was all the sensation from my uncle who was a great dancer while the gramophone played *One Two Cha Cha Cha* in the background.

The covered veranda became my father's music room during his 'guitar phase'. He sat on the steps for long hours, strumming the chords on summer evenings with the fan circling overhead, while I watched, fascinated. Dressed in a sleeveless cotton kurta and salwar, her long hair in a loose plait to one side, my mother's beaming face completed what is one of my most treasured childhood memories.

I remember her as an affectionate and playful young mother yet there was no casualness, no halfway measures, none of the easy-going attitude that one would expect from a teenaged girl. Her standards for herself were set high; she had to be the best at whatever she did. And with all her energies focused on me, she was a perfectly enthusiastic, fulltime mum.

She converted the backyard into a tiny personal zoo for me with white mice, birds, rabbits and a duck, which I spent hours chasing. My parents organized some spectacular birthday parties for me through my early childhood. It was a complete operation with my picture on the cover of the invites and each party planned around a special theme. The most delightful birthday present I ever got was a fluffy white puppy that arrived in a small cane basket. Dinky grew into a wonderfully handsome Pomeranian on whom we all doted.

My memories of my father are gentle. He was the kindest parent a child could have. 'Nelofar, wake up' – I can still hear his voice, as he woke me up for school. 'Look at the birds, they are calling you.' He would drive me down to Loreto Convent and there was always enough time for a few stories on the way. Somehow all his anecdotes seemed to involve tigers that he had encountered on hunting trips!

Living in a family home had had its advantages. The perks that came with being part of a joint family were taken for granted. Now, for the first time, my parents were coping with running an independent home and this brought with it some obvious issues. Money seemed to shrink faster than ever before and the end of the month was not a time they looked forward to.

One evening, Shahnaz and Nasir dressed up to go out for the evening. When they sat in the car my father noticed the needle of the fuel gauge on empty. They both searched their wallets; the situation in each was equally dismal. Shahnaz got out of the car and walked back to the house, all dressed up and looking miserable. Suddenly she heard the sound of a bell ringing. She looked through the window and was shocked to see my father on a bicycle, a huge smile on his face. 'Come on, Shunno,' he said. 'Let's go.'

'Where?' she asked. 'We have no money.'

'Which of your friends is the best cook?' he asked.

'Kamal Sidhu, for sure.'

'Well, it's dinner-time. Let's just drop in at her place.'

So she jumped up behind him, excited as a child, the wind blowing through her hair as they cycled through the empty roads of Lucknow.

Kamal Sidhu was happy to see her friends drop in unexpectedly. 'What a surprise!' she said. 'I have made some great biryani tonight.' After a few rehearsed expressions of formality, my parents happily agreed to stay for dinner.

Sometimes in life, less is more and the more you have the less you enjoy it. My mother remembers this as the most enjoyable evening out she has ever had.

Lucknow was a quiet, traditional town and the idea of women working was a fairly alien concept. Nevertheless, my spirited mother constantly looked around for an opportunity to occupy herself.

'Here, look at this,' said my father one morning as he pushed the paper towards her. In a tiny corner of the classifieds was an advertisement for a dress designer. Shahnaz's eyes sparkled at the thought of the opportunity and she gulped down her tea. It was a walk-in interview and she had no time to lose.

'I am getting ready, Tutu,' she said immediately.

'Are you sure you want to go for it?' he asked but his wife had already rushed off to dress for her first job interview.

Nari Kala Mandir was a small centre where women embroidered and stitched children's clothes. My mother, though completely untrained, applied for the job of a designer.

'What makes you think you will be able to style clothes when you have never studied fashion designing?' Mrs Mathur the head of the committee asked.

'I have a natural flair for anything artistic,' she claimed. 'And until you have tried me you will never know how good I am.'

Mrs Mathur smiled at her confidence. 'I like young people with enthusiasm,' she remarked. 'All right, Shahnaz, the job is yours.'

Her timings were fixed from nine to four and her salary at one hundred and seventy-five rupees a month.

'In what name would you want your salary cheque?' asked the old accountant, peering over his glasses that were perched on the tip of his nose.

'Ali Sahab,' my mother said politely, 'can you ask Mrs Mathur if I can take clothes for my daughter instead of my salary every month?'

'No salary, Shahnaz? Are you sure of that?' he asked in disbelief.

'Yes,' she replied. 'I love dressing her up more than anything in the world.'

Ali Sahab's stern face softened. For once he was touched by something other than figures. 'I will ask Madam and let you know.'

If I am ever asked what is the one thing I always want to remember about my mother, it is this: Even though it was a time in her life when she was short on finances, there was obviously no dearth of affection in her. I was her muse, her inspiration. I like to think that each time she designed an outfit she imagined me wearing it. My childhood photographs are almost all in fancy party frocks puffed with cancans, which were a must for me according to my designer, my mother.

The high point of those early years was when the Nari Kala Mandir needed to make its catalogue for an export enquiry and I was asked to be the model. My mother's designs on her favourite model – it could not have been a better match.

While my mother got busy with her new job I began spending the afternoons after school with my grandparents. Interestingly, my grandmother was very delicate and small built, not more than five feet and my grandfather was six feet three inches. Even so they were a made-for-each-other couple. My grandmother was so lovely and ethereal looking, it seemed to me as though she had just stepped off a cloud. Her skin was whiter than milk and her hair was silvery white as far as I can think back. She always wore crisp cotton saris, the loose end pulled carefully over her head and carried a small clutch. I would run out of school looking for her and the moment we spotted each other in the crowd our faces would spill over with smiles. I would then spend the afternoon in my grandmother's care, listening to stories of her days at Rahat Manzil in far-away Hyderabad and of her ancestors who had wielded swords and gone to war.

When evening drew near it brought with it a flurry of activity in the house. As the staff bustled about, I would sit, my eyes glued to the gate for the navy blue Austin coming down the driveway with a chauffeur and guard in traditional red livery. The doors of the car would open and a tall – taller than ever for me at that age – figure with a strong face and gentle eyes hidden behind horn-rimmed glasses would step out. A hush would fall over the house as though a lion had come into the vicinity, only to be broken as he walked in, calling for his '*dil ka tukra*'.

When he saw me, Nana's eyes would soften and a smile crease his face as the day's trials and tribulations at court melted away; he loved me enormously. He taught me about the oneness of religions, the importance of values and propriety and to respect all people. He was my hero and always will be. It was the years in my maternal grandparents' care that moulded me and I know so well that to have had those tiny grains of their character imbibed in me as a child was life's greatest and most silent event.

As a teenager, I remember joining Nana for his evening walk at Banjara Hills in Hyderabad where he had moved and hearing his inspirational words: 'Nelofar baby,' I remember him telling me, 'I think you should study to become a doctor. That's one profession that is needed everywhere. Even if your husband were living in a small town you would always find work if you were a doctor.'

Still every bit a women's libber, Nana was trying to ensure that his granddaughter as well became an independent-minded, career woman. Little did he realize then that his Chhoti Baby would grow to become a pioneer in her field and that I would stay by her side, protecting her and guiding her through her life, just as he had.

A Parisienne Model Appears in Lucknow

When I think back now, our days in Lucknow seem like a spellbound vacation in time. When my parents' lives were still encased in innocence, a time when they were taking their first tentative steps, waiting anxiously to explore the possibilities of life.

My mother had never worn a swimsuit in her life. Her mother had grown up in purdah and had curtains fitted in the cars her daughters rode in, so disrobing in public was a complete violation of her traditions. The Mohammad Bagh Club – the social hub of Lucknow's stylish set – had a beautiful covered pool that beckoned to Shahnaz. Her friends, Kanwal Sidhu and Gomti Vyas, swam on summer evenings, leaving my mother to flip through magazines on the deck while they frolicked in the water like dolphins.

'Come on, Shunno,' they would call out to her. 'We are having so much fun here.'

Initially, my mother declined but finally the peer pressure got to her. She could not bear to be the one left behind but neither was she willing to shed her mother's values. She finally found a way out. On a hot summer evening she emerged from the changing rooms wearing an ankle-length bathrobe over her swimsuit. To the utter shock of the other swimmers, she stepped into the pool with the robe still on.

For a few moments she stood in the water, wondering, what next? The robe was getting heavier by the minute and there was no way she could swim with it on. Finally, she took a deep breath and removed it, free at last to join her friends. Never having stepped into a pool, she couldn't swim at all, so while her friends swam to the deep end, she watched them sadly from the shallow waters.

The next day, my father spoke to the swimming coach who had a very novel method of teaching. He tied one end of a length of sturdy fabric around my mother's waist and held on to the other as he walked beside the pool – it must have been a sixties' thing because I have not seen this innovative method of teaching since. My mother flung her arms desperately to keep afloat. Every time she went down, the instructor would simply pull at the make-shift rope, ensuring she stayed afloat. It took a while but she ultimately joined her friends in the deep end with a triumphant smile.

'It doesn't matter what you want in life, it matters how badly you want it,' she has told me often. Her determined spirit was displaying itself in the smallest challenges; the deep end of the Mohammed Bagh club pool was just one of them.

The first glimmer of the star my mother was destined to be was seen at my father's youngest sister's wedding in Lucknow.

The shamiana was made from what seemed like miles of sweet-smelling juhi flowers. The men were dressed in sherwanis, as is the tradition with Muslims and the ladies, some of them in purdah, were in formal saris and ghararas. Abba and Amma were receiving their guests and at any point, one of their eight children stood by their side as part of the welcoming party.

In the middle of the staid and solemn nikah ceremony I suddenly saw my mother appear in a long, skin-hugging gold dress that flared out below the knees, making her look like a mermaid. A net veil draped her shoulders. Her long hair was swept into a sleek chignon. The effect was very dramatic. The dress was an adaptation of an evening gown that she had spent hours designing with her perplexed Lucknowi tailor.

I remember the flurry her entrance caused; my aunts rushing up to her with shocked expressions: 'What is this? Is that a *dress* you are wearing?' they asked with unconcealed horror.

'No,' she replied calmly. 'I am wearing a gharara but it's all in one piece.'

I stood beside her, wondering if she was in trouble but with my father giving her an approving smile she had little to worry about. He was always supportive of her, to the extent of being indulgent. The years between them gave her a slight edge and he would go to great lengths to see her aspirations realized.

At an age when other girls were wracked with self-doubt, Shahnaz stood, waiting to conquer the world, confident and beautiful, her signature style and unique persona shining through, even in small-town Lucknow.

My mother has always had a highly personalized style of dressing and even at the age of twenty-two she had a natural flair for unrivalled individuality; her versatility was not limited to the gold gharara. The fancy dress ball in Nainital where we vacationed in the early years was an opportunity for her to experiment with her creativity. I remember one summer when she dressed up as Cleopatra. With winged eyes and an artfully created serpent on her head she looked every bit the Egyptian queen. Another year, she went as Anarkali; it was a particularly eventful night because in her excitement she had left her veil in our cottage at the top of the mountain. Little did my father know that he would have to do more than just pretend to be Salim that night. Finding no other transport, he mounted a horse and being an excellent rider, galloped up the mountain and returned with the veil just in time for the show. Anarkali was delighted and beamed with relief.

One of my mother's hallmarks over the years has been the nose-pin she wears. She loves her sparkling stone and often, when the cameras are flashing, she requests photographers to shoot her from an angle where it can be seen. It was a hot summer day in Lucknow when she walked in and surprised her mother: 'Look, Mummy, look at my nose. I got it pierced.'

My grandmother looked at her and gasped: 'It's on the wrong side, you silly girl! It's always the right side that is pierced.'

'I know,' my mother replied with a twinkle in her eye. 'That's *why* I got the left side pierced.'

The early signs of a highly individualistic woman were emerging. Quintessentially Shahnaz – never one to conform, always making her own path; never one to follow, always the one to lead.

An Impulse to Chase Butterflies

Shahnaz sat by the Mohammad Bagh Club greens with a group of friends as Nasir played an energetic game of tennis. It was the beginning of winter. The knitting needles she held in her hands seemed to move with a life of their own as her eyes gazed ahead at an indistinct destiny.

The sound of her friends cheering made her aware that the game was over. A beaming Nasir walked over to Shahnaz with the swagger of a winner.

Though she tried to contain it, somewhere along the years a restlessness had taken grip of my mother's soul. She now felt the monotony of her blissful days – of the static life with few challenges and little struggle. She suffered from the discontent that is normally the hallmark of a person destined for success. It is an impulse, an inner voice, loud and strong within, even if the words are incomprehensible. Her latent, strongly motivated career-woman instinct was asserting itself.

Even though Lucknow was full of enchanted moments – of a life brimming with warm friends and the finer graces and a father who was in the top echelons of power – it failed to fulfil her aspirations. Nari Kala Mandir had had its day for her; working to earn a salary in 'frocks' for me had seemed fun for a while but that was nowhere close to where the young Shahnaz somehow sensed she was eventually destined to be.

One evening, when my mother entered my grandfather's house to pick me up, he noticed her unusually pensive mood.

'What is the matter with you, baby?' he asked in his usual gentle tone. 'Not feeling too well today?'

'Papa, I have been meaning to talk with you for some time now. I am bored with the way things are. I want to do something more than just design baby frocks and spend my evenings at the club. I know I can do so much more in life.'

Justice Beg looked at his daughter intently and saw his brilliant child restless, her talents wasted. He knew that Lucknow had its limits and that she needed to move on. He also realized that her lack of formal education would always be a stumbling block in her growth.

'Leave Nelofar with us and go to England to complete your education,' he said, hoping his daughter would find the courage to take a break and complete what he felt was the most important, unfinished part of her life.

But Shahnaz looked away – like she always did when she knew she was disappointing her father.

'I can't ever leave Tutu and go anywhere, Papa; and to leave Nelofar would be unthinkable.'

'You have so much of your mother in you,' her father said, accepting her decision with a soft smile and she knew that he had paid her the best compliment.

'Whatever I do, Papa, has to be with my family. They are an inseparable part of my life.'

Justice Beg was silenced by the loyalty of this young mother and wife. He wished in his mind that he had not given in; that he had not allowed Shahnaz to get married without completing her education. He was just getting his thoughts together when a blue Baby Hindustan, the latest in automobiles in the country, came down the driveway and my mother responded instinctively. Scooping me up in her arms with the nonchalance that only a mother can, she dashed to the waiting car, waving to her father. 'Bye Papa. Tutu is waiting. I have to go.'

Justice Beg remained troubled all evening as he pondered over his daughter's dilemma. At night he tossed and turned in bed hoping for an answer that would fulfil all his daughter's aspirations in one move. He was only too aware that behind the façade of her cheerfulness Shahnaz was still under deep pressure, coping with the expectations of the traditional family she had married into.

The next day, when his son-in-law drove up to the house to pick up his wife and daughter, Justice Beg waved him over. 'Come inside, Nasir,' he invited. 'Bibi has made some nice fish for you today.'

My father immediately got out of the car. 'Adab, Papa,' he said respectfully.

Justice Beg led his son-in-law to the white cane chairs placed in a neat circle on the soft grass. A tall pedestal fan stood nearby spreading the soothing fragrance of wet earth and the heady scent of the champa creeper. The table had been prepared for tea, with scones and deep-fried masala peas served in the floral-patterned china bowls that came out when special guests or the son-in-law visited. 'Nasir, have you ever thought of changing to a better job in the government?'

'Not really,' replied my father, not taking the question too seriously. 'I am happy with the job I have.'

'Well, I have been hearing a lot about the State Trading Corporation. I think it can open up many doors for you,'

'It will also mean that we would have to leave all of you and move to Delhi.'

'As much as we will miss you, I think it would be good for both you and Shahnaz. You are both young and Lucknow has its limitations. Besides, Shahnaz needs to continue her education and Delhi may open up her mind to different possibilities.'

'Leaving Lucknow is impossible for me. I don't want to leave my parents behind, especially now that Abba has retired and they too have settled down here. They would be terribly upset to see us go,' my father said as a gloved bearer walked in with the special river fish.

Justice Beg let the matter rest there; after all he was not going to interfere in his daughter's life beyond a point.

It took my mother some months to convince my father to break away from his roots and eventually he agreed to leave his hometown and his parents behind and take a step towards a new future. In fact, once his mind opened up to the idea, he was quite excited at the prospect of change. Yet there were many moments of angst that lay ahead when he tried to gently explain to Abba that he would be just an overnight train journey away; that he would visit Lucknow as often as he could. He was conditioned, more than any other role in life, to be a dutiful son and the move was not an easy one for him. Along with my mother he was also going through his own metamorphosis and she knew he had it in him to leave his family's protective cocoon for a more thriving and fulfilling life.

When my father's appointment to the most swank public sector organization of the time, the State Trading Corporation in New Delhi, finally came through, there was much celebration.

The night train to the capital was packed to capacity with the summer rush. Shahnaz and Nasir looked out of the window and waved to the family who had come to see them off. The stationmaster blew his sharp whistle, the engines were fired, the wheels turned and soon gained momentum. Shahnaz sat back and smiled, her eyes serene in the knowledge that this was one more journey ahead towards a more fulfilling life. Like a bird on her first flight she had fluttered her wings for long enough and she was now ready to soar; to discover her destiny.

In the sixties, Delhi was an urban village – a sprawling mass of scattered residential colonies, a far cry from the cosy warmth and charm of Lucknow. In the early days we missed our circle of security, our family and friends. It took us a while before we got used to the new city.

Our new home, E-117 Greater Kailash Part I, was chosen primarily because rents across the Defence Colony railway line were lower. The area was sparsely built and there were long tracts of empty land, giving it a strange, desolate feel. I missed the security of Lucknow most in the darkness of the night when the colony guard blew his sharp whistle and stamped his cane threateningly to ward off thieves. The idea of night-time bandits was very scary to me and my mother often had to carry me to her bed assuring me that I was safe. 'Mummy, let's go back to Lucknow,' I cried.

In the days to come my mother worked hard at creating a cosy home for us. The furniture from Lucknow was smartly re-upholstered to suit its change of residence and with my mother's inherent talent for giving every space her own touch, she picked up inexpensive cushions, lamps and accessories from that veritable treasure trove of New Delhi – Janpath – to give the house a warm and stylish feel.

My parents knew very few people in Delhi but gradually they started to move around and made some good friends. Mr and Mrs Sial and Mr and Mrs Mukherjee became their closest friends in Delhi and they spent many enjoyable evenings together.

Mrs Sial was a slim and elegant lady with a nonchalant attitude, quite the opposite of my mother, who was enthusiastic and excited about most things. Mrs Mukherjee, on the other hand, was a plump Bengali lady with glowing skin and an infectious sense of humour. Together they provided the initial support system that my mother relied on for advice and a sense of reassurance while facing the challenges that came with making a home in a new city without her family to lean on.

Mrs Sial and my mother often met in the mornings for coffee and chat sessions. I remember returning home from school one day and hearing strange sounds coming from her room. Curious, I walked in and to my utter horror saw my mother and her friend sitting with some icky stuff on their upper lip that to me looked like a moustache mould. They were screeching in pain as they tried to rip it off their faces. I ran out, confused and terrified. Later, my mother told me that women in Delhi didn't like facial hair, so one of the big city girls was teaching them how to remove it.

'But Mummy, you have no facial hair to start with,' I said, looking at her perfect, rose-hued, porcelain skin.

I was enrolled in the first standard at Summer Fields School nearby. Bua – the trusted maid my grandmother had sent with us along with innumerable instructions – took me to school and picked me up as well. I missed my grandmother most in the afternoons when I remembered her waiting to take me home in the blue Austin that had somehow begun to feel like a loyal friend.

For a family that had lived in large homes with lavish gardens, the house at E-117 Greater Kailash, felt small and claustrophobic. Built on a tiny plot with houses on both sides it seemed like basic accommodation and nothing more. So one of the enterprises my mother took on was to find a nicer house for us to live in. On one of her exploratory trips around the colony she spotted a to-let board hanging from the first floor of a large, two-storeyed house facing a park with a hillock and a beautiful temple built on it. So spectacular and calm was the view from this home that it looked like a scenic picture postcard. She knew that it was way beyond our budget, yet she opened its gates and walked in confidently.

The owner of W-33, Mrs Gupta, was an amiable lady who politely informed my mother that she had already received several excellent offers for her house and had no plans of renting it out for less. But my mother refused to accept her words of refusal as a closed door. She visited Mrs Gupta every day and chatted with her for hours, enthralling her with stories of her mother's youth in Rahat Manzil and her aristocratic lineage. Finally, Mrs Gupta gave in – the charming girl had completely won her over. She persuaded her husband to let us have the place even if it meant getting a little less rent. The early signs of an enigmatic and determined personality were beginning to display themselves in her life. As she often says: 'It doesn't matter what you want in life, it matters how badly you want it.'

Moving to W-33 brought a lot of happiness to my parents' lives. The rooms of the new house were spacious, with long windows that let in the sunlight. They often sat out on the balcony facing the lit-up temple on the hillock, just soaking in the serenity of the view. My school was just a stone's throw away, across the muddy patch that later became a children's park and I would run down with Bua chasing me, just in time for class every morning.

Delhi was a city of long distances and poor public transport, so my parents soon bought a snazzy, red-and-white Standard Herald. The car had individual bucket seats in the front with a space in between just large enough for me to wedge myself into.

My father started taking my mother for driving lessons in the mornings; he was an excellent teacher but she was not the best student. She drove too fast and without any sense of timing, giving my father and me absolute nightmares. My mother still is, undoubtedly, the worst driver I have ever encountered.

Yet, with a huge 'L' hanging on the car to absolve her of any responsibility, wielding her learner's licence, she scoured the endless roads of Delhi without fear or hesitation, even navigating her way through the chaotic traffic of Old Delhi for an exploratory trip. When my father heard of her adventures, he was aghast but my mother beamed with a sense of victory. She loved the high that came with achieving the impossible. She had no desire to live her life on the banks of a pond when she could explore the tempestuous waves of the ocean.

My mother was still waiting to exhale – she had not been able to let go of her quest; her search for herself was leading her from one centre of learning to another.

She experimented with innumerable courses in search of a vocation that would be in perfect consonance with her intellect. Interior decoration, cookery, painting – just about everything was tried out. I actually have this vivid memory of my mother making perfect swirls in hot oil on the day she was taught how to make jalebis. Then there were the art classes, where she developed a penchant for Batik. All her saris were enthusiastically turned into objets d'art, hanging from the first floor balcony to dry, shimmering in the bright, exquisitely vibrant colours that she, with her free-spirited nature, always selected.

Yet none of these pursuits brought her satisfaction. Her true calling eluded her. She was still restless.

Aruna and Saeed Naqvi were close friends of my parents and on one of their informal evenings together my mother happened to mention how terribly, terribly bored she was.

'I have done everything under the sun, Saeed,' she said. 'But nothing seems to hold my interest for long.'

Saeed turned around and said the magic words that were to change her life forever: 'Why don't you try studying beauty therapy?' He gave her the address of a friend who conducted classes and said, 'Give it a try.'

It was a casual suggestion and having made it he moved on with his life – but hers would never be the same again.

The tiny scrap of paper with the address of a beauty school conducted out of a room at a lady's house in Delhi was the first step to my mother's magnificent destiny.

She enrolled herself at Mrs Chatterji's beauty school and within a few days was completely enthralled by her work, reading through piles of books with keen interest.

'*This* is going to be my career, Tutu,' she told my father emphatically.

She had finally discovered her talent; one that would possess her for the rest of her life. She would one day be called a crusader and be honoured by dozens of nations. The world would give her a standing ovation – but success does not come easily. There would be many hurdles on the way; there would be innumerable bridges she would have to cross before she would achieve success. Mrs Chatterji's beauty school was just the beginning of her journey. Her interest in her chosen profession was so deep and sincere that she started considering the possibility of going abroad to study her subject further.

'I want to go to London to study beauty therapy,' she told my father.

'Why?' he asked, confused. 'You have just finished a course with a competent instructor, what *more* do you want to learn?'

'I want to learn the latest techniques at the best schools in the world. I want to be the best in whatever I do, Tutu.'

The importance of education had been so deeply ingrained in my mother's mind that this seemed the natural course to take. She had never lacked in energy and drive and she did not believe in compromise. She was a traveller in quest; the next phase of her journey was essential to her growth as a professional and as a human being. She knew it in her bones that it was time to move ahead again and she sensed the same restlessness that had besieged her that day in Lucknow, when she realized that the place had given her all it could.

My father was confused by the extent of her desire to pursue what he considered a means to break the monotony of her days, while my mother clearly felt the need to enhance her education; to simply be extraordinary in everything she did. My father aimed for reasonable progress and a good life for his family; he was not in sync with the idea of pursuing what he felt were utopian dreams. It was difficult for him to comprehend what she was searching for. He was calm and peaceful, she was effervescent and driven. He believed in being content with his blessings, she had an impulse to move ahead with him; to make a bid for the seemingly impossible. Yet he loved her so unconditionally that he would always move over to her side and make all her plans and her deepest wishes come true. He had it in him to become her greatest support, to become the means of her journey ahead by holding her hand and leading her to her destinations.

My father also sensed that her commitment to their relationship remained unquestionable at all times and he spent many sleepless nights before arriving at what seemed like the perfect solution: a foreign posting. The State Trading Corporation had offices in many parts of the world and he began looking for the right opportunity. He discussed his plans with my mother and she was instantly optimistic. Essentially a traditional woman, she saw this as the best way to keep her family together and pursue the education she yearned for. But they both knew that Abba would react strongly to the move. He had always insisted that all his children remain close to him.

Tradition and emancipation clashed once again when Justice Beg declared that if Shahnaz could not go along with her husband on a foreign posting and study, he would send her alone. This time my mother accepted her father's decision and I think her stand helped push the course of events in the right direction. It took innumerable trips to Lucknow and all my father's skills of persuasion to make Abba appreciate that my mother's education was essential to maintain the harmony in their relationship. It was the toughest exercise that he ever undertook and he looked distraught and guilty for several weeks as Abba declined his permission.

My paternal grandfather stepped back finally, realizing that his stance was causing a great deal of unhappiness to his children. Finally, one day my father came home beaming. 'Shunno,' he said. 'Where do you want to go – Tehran or Cairo?' He had been offered a choice between the two cities.

After much thought, my parents chose Tehran, the Paris of the East. For my mother it was a concrete step towards achieving her dreams. Her focus was clear; she had her sights set on a star but she knew it was not going to come down for her. She now made up her mind to stretch herself to her limits and pluck it from the sky.

A Bird in the Sky

The Air India jet circled over the city of Tehran, blowing giant rings of white smoke into the clouds. My stomach was churning with excitement and anxiety as I looked down at what was to be our new home. Shimmering lights dotted the ground below. The neon lights created strange movements of colour and the silhouettes of the snow-capped mountains bordering the city gave the landscape a strange, ethereal look. To my young mind, it was like descending on Fairyland. I looked at my parents and saw them both smiling.

As we were to find out soon enough, Tehran had all the glitz and glamour of a European city along with the warmth and friendliness that can be found only in the East. It had more than its share of natural beauty with long avenues lined with tall chinar trees and brooks rippling through the city, making the most soothing music I had ever heard. The water in these brooks flowed down from the snow-capped peaks and was as clear as the most perfect crystal. It was common to see people bending down and cupping their hands to drink the cool, sparkling elixir.

Once we had absorbed the initial enchantments of the city, my parents got down to the job of finding a house. Tehran stands on a slope in a valley from where one can see snow-peaked mountains all around. The northern part of the city, which lies on the elevated slopes of the mountains, is called Shemran. In the days when the country was still a monarchy the magnificent structure of the Royal Palace defined the area as the upper crust neighbourhood.

My father was entitled to a fairly large villa and we were free to choose one of the charming old structures with pools and apple orchards as our new home. It took a lot for my mother to overcome the temptation to live in the beautiful environs of Shemran and settle for a sleek, modern house in the centre of the city.

She was not here for an extended vacation, she reminded herself and us; she would be joining classes and it would not make sense for her to live so far out of the city in an area from where commuting would be difficult.

We were the first tenants of the house on Avenue Jamshedabadé Shomali. The home smelt new with freshly painted walls, its focal point being a glazed atrium with a small garden and a fish-pond in the centre of the home. My mother had always had a way with spaces and our house in Tehran became an exotic showcase for the Indian artifacts that she had carried with her. My parents had been asked to take their furniture from India and my mother had carefully designed every piece; pleased that she was able to do this on government expense.

Being the head of the Indian trade mission in Tehran was the high point of my father's career. He took to Iran like a fish to water. He spoke Persian comfortably and his intelligence, his disarming smile and his ready wit made the Indian government millions in successful deals. He had a reputation for never returning with a negative answer. Soon enough my father had

93

made inroads into every department in the Iranian government, enhancing trade between the two countries like never before. He revelled in this phase of his life. It was a time when my mother had yet to make her mark in the world, while my father's professional success made him shine brighter than he ever would with her by his side.

One of the first social events my parents were invited to in Tehran was the opening of the Air India office. Initially, my mother was overwhelmed by the prospect of rubbing shoulders with women dressed in Armani and Christian Dior. But her natural confidence soon took over and she began assembling her outfit for the gala night – a diamante trimming bought from a local fabric store was converted into a choker to be worn around her neck, this was paired with a golden sari with pink polka dots. I remember admiring her with girlish awe and pride as she waltzed out of the room looking dazzling, her burgundy tresses flowing down her back, when she left for the party that night. I was sure she would be the star of the night and I was right.

The next morning's papers spoke of Nasir Husain's vivacious wife, who had worn pink diamonds to the opening of the Air India offices. The glimmer of a woman less ordinary was apparent to all; Armani and Dior paled in comparison as she traipsed past them with the natural grace and ease of a woman born to win.

Before long, my parents became a popular couple on the party circuit in Tehran and our garden came alive every few months with a guest list that included diplomats and top government brass. My father was a great host and aware of his guests' preferences, he kept a full bar in the house though he never touched a drop of alcohol himself. The cultural roots of our family were so deep and strong that even though we had left India, the fragrance of the land we loved still lingered in our home. We managed to retain the ethos that we were born into.

One of the more eventful parties given by my parents was in honour of the British military attaché and his wife.

After days of careful planning, the theatre of the evening finally began to play out when the guests started to arrive in their glistening limousines. Each table set out on the lawns was lit with tall white candles and decked with sprays of seasonal flowers carefully chosen by my mother. The evening had all the elements necessary for a memorable party. Warsi, our gifted cook who had come with us from Lucknow, could single-handedly serve up a delectable feast for a hundred people and tonight he had outdone himself. Guests gushed over the cuisine and the divine flavours, anointing him as a gastronomical ambassador for India.

Lying in my bed with the lights put out I could hear the sound of music filtering in and I could almost visualize the small band as they played a musical medley of the latest hits of the time – 'Sugar Sugar' and 'Strangers in the Night'.

Unable to sleep, I walked up to the glazed windows and peeped through the curtains at the starry night outside. The guest of honour was walking towards my mother and bowing politely.

'Shahnaz,' the attaché said. 'May I have the pleasure of this dance?'

When my mother did not move, he looked at her, confused.

'I only dance with my husband,' she finally said.

Mr Prince, the attaché, smiled, amused and took it with the kind of humour that only the British can manage. This was a statement she repeated quite often to the many men who approached her at parties, always much to their embarrassment. I cannot help but mention here that my father spent most of his time at social gatherings dancing with his wife and growing daughter. I remember frantically searching him out at a nightclub as a teenager and dragging him to the dance floor, saying, 'Come on, Papa, they're playing my favourite number.'

The party in Tehran that night had more amusing moments. After it wrapped up in the wee hours of the morning, my exhausted and relieved parents walked into their bedroom ready to fall into bed. But as they opened the door and switched on the light, my mother let out a scream. To their utter shock they saw one of their guests sprawled across their bed in blissful slumber. Obviously, he had enjoyed Indian hospitality in excess. My father frowned, not quite approving of the dishevelled man occupying his bed. My parents slept in the guest room that night, after my father instructed Warsi to serve the guest breakfast in the morning. However, before the household woke up, the gentleman vanished into the night, never to be seen again.

One of my proudest moments as a youngster was when I was in school in Tehran. The bell rang as classes for the day got over and the children raced towards the gates and the real world waiting outside. Never pushy or aggressive by nature, I was walking slowly down the path, dragging my bag behind me, when I heard a bunch of kids screaming hysterically: 'Raj Kapoor is here, Raj Kapoor is here!'

Energized, I ran to the gate and pushed through the wildly excited crowd but when I saw the man they were calling 'Raj Kapoor' I could not believe my eyes.

'That's my dad!' I screamed proudly, loud enough for the world to hear. With a crowd of shocked kids watching, I strutted to the waiting white stretch Chevrolet and proudly parked myself next to my father. When the car pulled away, I waved from the window to the awestruck crowd, a huge happy grin on my face.

Those were some of the most wonderful days we spent as a family. We shared a special relationship, the kind that is forged when a family is huddled together abroad. The pressures of extended family ties, obligations and duties vanished temporarily and though the price was being away from those dear to us, anyone who has lived away from home for a while will agree how emotionally liberating it can be. This was also a time when the stress that comes with business and success was still at bay. It was a time in our lives when we held hands and saw a perfect world together.

Weekend vacationing was a national obsession in Iran and my parents and I often went on trips outside the city; we would drive to the ski slopes in the winters, or to the Caspian Sea in the summers in just a few hours. On weekends we normally went on short trips to the beach with my parents' friends, Aziz and Esther in their swank new Mercedes Benz. Aziz had a passion for cars; it seemed as though driving was second nature to him. The drive took us through sloping valleys and mountains and a nine-kilometre long tunnel through Mt Damaband, an inactive volcano. It was on our way back from one of these trips that we had a proverbial brush with destiny.

As we were nearing Tehran on our return, we could spot the city lights twinkling in the distance and we felt the relief that comes with sighting the first signs of home at the end of a journey. Even though he wasn't at the wheel, my father was alert as always and he suddenly felt the car moving towards the edge of the cliff instead of the curving mountain road. He instantly realized that Aziz had fallen asleep while driving and in a fraction of a second he grabbed the steering wheel and manoeuvred the car back on the road, just in time to avoid a terrible accident.

All's well that ends well. We stopped for a cup of tea, still shaken by the experience. There was a profound silence, a moment of stillness as each one of us seemed to thank the omnipresent hand that had protected us. The Gods had still so much planned for us. My sun-tanned young mother had yet to keep her date with destiny. I often wonder if it was the compelling force of her kismet that saved us that day. And of course, the fact that I had to live to tell the story of a family kissed by magic.

While in Tehran my mother often looked out anxiously for the postman, waiting for a letter from home. When she recognized her father's monogrammed envelope she would tear it open excitedly and sit down with it, reading and re-reading every bit of news it carried. One day, my mother tore open a letter with the usual excitement that came with receiving an envelope addressed by a familiar hand. The calligraphic handwriting of her brother, Wally, was unmistakable.

'I have finally got my P-form to travel out of India,' Wally had written. 'I am going to take a trip to London to see if I would like to settle there. I cannot resist stopping by and meeting all of you.'

My mother could barely contain her happiness at the thought that her brother was going to visit and began to make plans to make his stay interesting. On the night that Wally arrived, a small group of friends was invited over to meet him. One of the invitees was the head of a large British infrastructure company and Wally and he talked all evening. When he was leaving, he dropped his card in Wally's hand and said, 'Come and see me tomorrow morning. If I can tempt you with a good enough offer, I do hope you will consider taking it up.'

Wally debated the next morning. He was very keen on settling in England. Two of his cousins, Khusro and Rasheed Beg, had moved to Canada and the U.S. and had done exceedingly well there. The West was now beckoning him.

'Why don't you just meet him and see what he has to offer? You don't have to take it up if you don't want to,' my father suggested. Wally met Peter Haze at his office the next day and stayed on in Tehran. His ticket for his onward journey to London expired in time and he lived in the annexe of our house for the next few years.

Every major international beauty school was represented in Tehran and my mother enrolled herself in the best courses that were offered during our four-year stay there. She spent long hours expanding her knowledge base, learning the latest techniques in the beauty business and striving to be the best at whatever she did. The curative aspects of beauty care, those involving the treatment of problems like acne, premature ageing, skin pigmentation, hair loss and other para-medical issues interested her immensely. She also became aware of the interdependence between the treatment methods and the creams and lotions that would give the best results. To be in control of the ingredients she would use on her clients and to assure them the most effective treatments she decided to join Lean of Copenhagen, a well-known school of cosmetology run by a Danish lady. The courses at the beauty schools were expensive. My father, being on a government salary, could ill-afford the astronomical fees; the financial strain of managing the mounting bills was increasing. It was quite clear that my mother needed to find a source of income to fund her education. One day, she was chatting with her friends in the neighbourhood and they mentioned that the school down the road needed an English teacher.

'Shahnaz, your English is so good. You will get the job for sure,' said Farishthae, a close friend.

It seemed like the perfect opportunity, so my mother dressed up in her most elegant clothes and went for an interview. While she waited for her turn, she chatted with the other applicants and noticing their uncomfortable, halting English she was quite sure that she would get the job. Finally it was her turn.

'Where do you come from?' asked the bespectacled principal.

'I come from India, Madam.'

'Oh, India. Many wild animals there. Tigers, elephants, I believe.'

'Yes but they are in the jungles and we don't get to see them much.'

'So, you went to school in India?'

'Yes, I did. I went to St. Mary's Convent, which is a very good missionary school. In fact it was run by Irish nuns,' she said with a hint of pride in her voice.

'Ah, that's why you speak such good English.'

'Thank you, Ma'am,' my mother replied, an optimistic smile on her face. 'In fact an essay of mine was chosen to be circulated in schools in England.'

'And where did you graduate from?'

My mother held her breath, she felt her heart racing. It was the moment she had been dreading. 'I have not done my graduation,' she replied.

The elderly lady put the résumé down abruptly and looked at the anxious girl in front of her. 'It seems you were not told that all applicants must at least be graduates.'

My mother came home looking grim and disappointed, her father's words echoing in her head. 'Baby, you can't go through life without a proper education.' At some level she had thought that even though she had not been to college, her experiences down the path of life would be recognized. She had never doubted her ability yet the lack of a college degree had never confronted her so bluntly before.

My mother's inability to find a job that would support her education frustrated her. She tossed and turned every night, searching for a solution. And then one evening, she found her answer at a party where she was conversing with a gentleman who had just launched the *Tehran Tribune*, the city's first English magazine. He was an enterprising American who wanted to fill the gap for an English news journal in Tehran but was faced with the daunting dilemma of finding good English writers.

Shahnaz smelt an opportunity.

'Do you need writers for your magazine?' she asked hopefully.

'Yes,' said the gentleman. 'I am desperately looking for people who can write well in English.'

'I am sure I could write some good pieces for you,' she volunteered.

'What can you write on?' he asked.

'Beauty, humour, short stories. Just about anything,' she said excitedly.

The next morning she was sitting in the offices of the *Tehran Tribune*, waiting to meet the editor.

Will he ask me if I am a graduate? she wondered nervously as she took the chair for the interview.

'I have been going through the two pieces you sent ahead and I must say I am very impressed. I would be most happy if you would write for our journal,' he said.

My mother smiled broadly, unable to conceal her relief at finally being given the opportunity to earn and support her studies. For the next three years, Shahnaz almost single-handedly kept the *Tehran Tribune* afloat, writing under four different names: Shahnaz, Nelofar, Khursheed – the second name given to her at birth – and Talat, which is my second name. Her imagination and her prolificness were astonishing as was her drive to make things happen. Hammering away on the heavy Remington typewriter into the early hours of the morning, she wrote short stories, political commentary, humorous pieces and articles on beauty. Each word was money in her pocket and she typed till her fingers were raw.

My father was alarmed to see her typing away with bandaged fingers one night, a look of grim determination on her face. 'Take a break,' he told her. 'You can't go on like this.' But from the look in her eyes he knew that she had overcome her physical pain with her indomitable will to support her education.

My mother had set her sights on Helena Rubinstein's institute in London. She had been inspired by the legendary cosmetician and industrialist and Rubinstein's centre in London had become an aspirational landmark for her. Her trips to London to study at the world's premier institute of its time became a regular feature for many months. While she was there, she stayed with Justice Dhawan, India's ambassador to the United Kingdom.

Ironically, my grandfather had been offered ambassadorship to the U.K. but had declined the offer since his ascetic lifestyle was not in sync with the social life of a diplomat; instead he had suggested Justice Dhawan for the job. My mother was extremely disappointed that her father had refused such an amazing opportunity but Justice Beg never doubted his decision. On his part, Justice Dhawan was always happy to welcome the daughter of his mentor into his house.

My mother's time in England enriched her knowledge and experience. It also exposed her to the detrimental effects of chemicals. An incident that impacted her strongly and guided the focus of her career plan was a chance meeting with a girl who often visited the Helena Rubinstein centre in London for treatment of a crop of pimples on her face. One day the girl walked in guided by her mother who, distraught as she was, explained that her daughter had damaged her eyesight using a chemically-laden mascara that promised instantly thick lashes. Her case shocked my mother and she resolved to look for a natural substitute to every beauty problem when she returned to India.

On her return from the Rubinstein institute my mother had the confidence she needed to set up her first small salon at home in Tehran. Unfortunately, for me, I paid the price for her first venture. There were no spare rooms in the house, so I packed up my rows of dolls and belongings and moved into my parents' room. I had seen the bandages on my mother's fingers, I knew how hard she had worked and I wanted to support her in whatever way I could. The salon was very successful and over time she built an exclusive list of clientele who came to her regularly by appointment.

Four years after we arrived in Tehran, my father's achievements were rewarded with every officer's dream – a posting to Paris. I was thrilled to bits at the thought of turning into a teenager in Paris, meeting my first romance under the Eiffel Tower, strolling along the banks of the Seine. But that was not to be. My parents were homesick by then and my mother's instinct told her that it was the perfect time for her to launch her career in India. She had a natural flair for business and her decision to let go of an opportunity to be hosted by the government for four years in Paris showed how serious the young entrepreneur was.

At times, I wonder what would have happened if she had chosen Paris over India. Four years would have been enough time for her to launch her career from the fashion and beauty capital of the world. She might even have been the greatest Indian export of the pre-infotech days. But that was not part of her plan. Anybody who is familiar with the course her life has taken would know that my mother's dreams were always rooted in India. Not once did her ambition lead her to look for success abroad. Her reasons for leaving India were purely to educate herself at the best beauty schools. Armed with the knowledge and skills required to succeed, she returned to her own country.

Even though our time in Tehran had been a wonderful experience, moving back home to India brought with it a sense of absolute joy for all of us, accompanied with the sense of peace that one experiences when one returns to one's roots. As the aircraft hovered over New Delhi, my parents smiled in anticipation of meeting the family after what had been a long separation. My father's parents, Abba and Amma, with my uncles, aunts and cousins, had all converged in Delhi to receive us with marigold garlands. Abba was pleased at being reunited with his son; he had not relished the thought of him leaving his side for so long. It was a wonderful and warm homecoming. My mother's parents waited for her to visit them in Hyderabad, where they had moved after my grandfather's retirement.

We returned to Greater Kailash once more; this time to the top floor of M-92, as a stop-gap measure, till we found a house we could live in permanently. It had the comfort of being close to our old home at W-33 and had the familiar view of the temple and hillock but from a different perspective.

It was all so good, yet it seemed inconceivable at the time to imagine that there were forces at work that would change this picture-perfect story.

Banjara Hills

Shahnaz's beautiful mother shook her head, confounded by her youngest child's drive – nothing could tie Shahnaz down to traditional matrimony. Sayeeda Begum realized that her daughter was now beyond her control and was astutely charting her future with her wonderful husband. At least she had been right on one issue. Nasir was the perfect match for her. He loved her, cherished her and at every point was her greatest support. Sayeeda Begum was happy that in many ways Shahnaz had steered her life on course with her aspirations.

My grandparents were impressed with the way their daughter had educated herself while preserving the values and traditions she had been taught; holding her family sacred and yet challenging the traditional image of the woman she was expected to be.

A woman has no battles to fight if she celebrates her womanhood in its completeness. If she remembers that Nature chose her as the giver of life so her abilities of heart and mind, her judgement and instincts, are finely tempered to meet any challenge. My mother had merged her family life with her ambitions and was at peace with herself as a parent, as a wife and as an aspiring professional.

Banjara Hills, Hyderabad – where my grandparents had returned to live after my grandfather had retired as Chief Justice of UP – was an emotive stop-over between one phase in my mother's life and the next. Bonding with the family was important to her and she took time off from her rigorous journey to the top of the world to become one with her roots again. It was also a pilgrimage to pay obeisance to the man she worshipped.

Her father wore an expression of unalloyed happiness as he greeted his daughter; as though his soul were finally at peace. His hopes of making his daughter economically independent seemed well on their way to fruition. Maybe sending her to Cambridge as he had wanted was not quite realistic considering the times but in spite of an early marriage and becoming a mother at sixteen, she had managed to change the course of her life. He was proud she had it in her to struggle and engage herself in life as though it were an arena.

Our first few weeks in Hyderabad were enlightening for me.

'I want you to recognize yourself here, Nelofar. I want you to always remember where you came from. This is the city that will always remind you of your great heritage,' my mother told me as she took me to the city's museums and narrated its history and the life of her great-grandfather, Sir Afsar Ul Mulk, whose image I was intrigued to see imprinted on Canadian stamps. I was also fascinated by the photographs of him with King George on a hunting trip in India and my all-time favourite – a picture of him feeding tea to his horse from a porcelain cup. In a world consumed with female beauty it was interesting that the family was known for the best looking men.

My great-grandfather was a man of strong convictions and had the courage to have his own grave built in his lifetime. He would lie in the white marble chamber and meditate every day. Surrounded as he was by constant adulation, he said that meditating in his final resting place was a humbling experience that put into perspective who he was and connected his soul to the hereafter.

When he was struck by paralysis in his later years, he went into seclusion in a part of Rahat Manzil that was cordoned off. Here he was cared for by a loyal attendant. His family and his children were then never allowed to see him again. It was his wish that he should always be remembered as he had been and that sentiment was respected. He neither aged, nor faded away; he simply walked off the stage, a brave and handsome man.

It was in Hyderabad that my mother finally found the key to her success, a discovery that translated into a business idea that has caught the imagination of generations of Indian women. Sitting with her family on the sprawling lawns of Banjara Hills, she fiddled distractedly with the clipboard that lay on her lap, considering and rejecting ideas, scribbling a multitude of names that she kept striking out impatiently. She had spent four long years working hard to educate herself and learn the latest techniques from the best beauty schools in the world, yet there was something missing. She needed something exceptional that would set her new business apart from the rest. She was sure that she would only stay with natural products but she needed to give her nebulous thoughts concrete shape. She looked up from her clipboard and noticed her mother's radiant face glowing in the light of the evening sun. How perfectly lovely she was.

'Mummy, I have never seen such perfect skin as yours. In all the skin-care centres abroad, of all the women I have met from every part of the world, you have the best skin.'

Looking at her mother's complexion through the newly trained eyes of a skin specialist, Shahnaz could not but help compare the luminous lustre of Sayeeda's porcelain complexion with the sunburnt, tired complexions of Westerners. It was not just their demanding lifestyles but also their method of caring for themselves that was different. They suffered from chemical fatigue; every time they applied a lotion or cream, they loaded their skins with strong, often toxic, elements.

Sayeeda Begum smiled bashfully. 'You see me through a daughter's eyes.'

'Honestly, Mummy. What *do* you use?'

'Just a few things that your grandmother taught me; the Rahat Manzil beauty routine.'

My mother was surprised. 'I have been travelling all over the world, spending so much time and money studying beauty, when the secret lies with you, right here in my family.' She had finally found the missing link; ancient, homegrown beauty cures that had been sifted through time and perfected through the ages were going to be her consuming passion.

The next morning she woke up, ready to take lessons from her mother. She made a list of all the ingredients her mother used, assembled them around her and then listened attentively as Sayeeda explained the intricate treatments and the reasons behind using certain herbs instead of others. My mother was fascinated, making notes, observing, asking occasional questions. There were remedies for hair growth, dry lips, prickly heat, even a hair fragrance for added allure. One of the recipes required soaking rice and four other ingredients in water for forty days with rose petals. The water had to be drained and fresh, fragrant rose petals added every day. The goodness and medicinal value of forty rounds of fresh petals made the mixture a potent beauty aid. Today the well-packaged product with a few modifications is an all-time company hot seller. Shahnaz had discovered a new dimension to her career plans; one that made her feel good about its purity. While studying in London she had realized the answer to human wellness and care lay with Nature, not with synthetic chemicals. She rang up my father to tell him that she was extending her stay in Hyderabad because she wanted to spend some time researching India's rich medicinal history.

My father was very encouraging and told her to take as long as she needed. He asked her if, in the meantime, he should move to a nice set of furnished rooms that he had found.

'It comes with staff, it is something like a service apartment and is perfect for a short stay while we search for a house,' he said enthusiastically. Once my mother agreed, he moved all our belongings from the top floor of M-92 to the smartly decorated accommodation at B-52 Greater Kailash and waited for us to return.

My mother began to read books on Ayurveda and visited Vedic specialists to assimilate and imbibe their knowledge. She found herself profoundly engrossed in the study of this timeless science, learning ancient methods and formulations that focused on skin and hair problems, so that she could offer her clientele natural substitutes to counter every beauty problem. She found the Indian science compelling and recognized its untapped potential. However, she was surprised to find that Ayurveda had been completely ignored in India; the immense accumulation of years of knowledge had remained neglected, waiting to be rediscovered in the very country of its origin.

What was even more surprising was the response she got when she questioned women about their beauty routine. Most of them relied on uninspiring local brands. There was not a single product at the time in the Indian market that was geared towards serious skin-care. Some 'lucky' ones waited for family members to visit from other parts of the world bringing back imported creams and lotions with them. As for having a weekly facial, very few women knew such a thing existed.

It was going to be an up-hill journey. She would have to convince a generation of women fascinated with foreign products to try the natural goodness of Ayurveda and awaken them to the concept of regular skin-care. But Shahnaz's confidence left no room for self-doubt. She could have taken a franchise from any one of the foreign establishments where she had studied and cashed in on a ready clientele that was all too eager to lap up anything Western. Instead, my mother decided to swim against the tide. It was a decision fraught with risk but then in Robert Frost's immortal words, she 'took the one less travelled by/ And that has made all the difference.'

The House Destiny Chose

Did any of the women who made it to the top plan it that way? Anita Roddick and Helena Rubinstein were self-made women with tremendous drive but could they have predicted the extent of their success? Did my mother imagine that she would be one of the beauty divas of her time?

Not really.

What she had wanted was to start a very exclusive salon where she would meet people by appointment and make creams and lotions for individual skin and hair problems. She had never planned on being anywhere close to where she reached.

My mother's natural business instincts made her all too aware of the fact that when starting a new business the importance of the perfect location could not be underestimated. It plays a vital role in the success or failure of an enterprise and a lot of care and thought is needed to make the right choice. She spent long hours agonizing over the perfect spot but ultimately it was fate that led her to it, saying, 'Not there but here. *This* will be the perfect place for you.'

Positioning herself in an upmarket area of the city was essential to convey an image of exclusivity and after some research she selected Westend as the ideal neighbourhood. After days of laboriously searching through the Sunday advertisement columns and meeting property agents with my father, she finally found just what she was looking for – a modern, newly-built villa in Westend that would be both home and salon. The only thing that stood in her way was the unaffordable rent. She took a flight back to Hyderabad to speak with her father who indulgently dug into his savings and gave her the funds she needed.

My mother returned to Delhi the very next day, eager to start work on India's most exclusive beauty salon. My parents met the landlord and the rent was settled. They agreed to pay the advance and sign the lease the following day. My mother was thrilled; she couldn't wait to get the keys of their new home in her hands; but fate had other plans.

Since they had an early morning appointment with the landlord, my parents withdrew the money from the bank and kept it at home that evening.

The family woke up the next morning to the maid's hysterical cries. 'Help, someone help!' The cries grew louder and shriller by the moment.

'What's happened?' my father demanded as he rushed out of the bedroom with my mother and I following him.

My knees buckled when I saw the scene of destruction. Our bags and belongings had been ripped open and strewn all over the backyard. My parents were stunned.

'Tutu,' my mother called out to him holding up an empty bag. 'Tutu, they took all the money! They took the money for our dream home.'

She had faced every challenge life had thrown at her, worked her way up every gruelling step and travelled the world with a guardian angel by her side. It seemed ironical that her world

Adorable at two

Letting her hair down

A stylish schoolgirl

A young lady at fifteen

With her 'cardboard crown' in Mussoorie

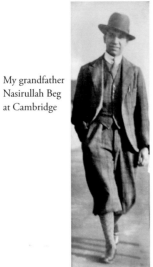

My grandfather
Nasirullah Beg
at Cambridge

Just married : Sayeeda & Nasirullah Beg

The Begs': a family portrait

My grandfather, Chief Justice Beg with President Radhakrishnan

Mirza Vilayat Ali Beg

Osman Yar Ud Daula

Three generations of Commander-in-Chiefs of the
Hyderabad Army and Sir Afsar-Ul-Mulk on horseback

Sir Afsar-Ul-Mulk
on a Canadian stamp

Sir Afsar
looks on as
King George
wades the
river with
the help
of a sepoy.

The
family
table at
Rahat
Manzil

Encouraging women's emancipation: Sir Afsar blessing his granddaughters before a sword fencing match, so they could play with dolls & swords with the same ease

Mum with her doll. The picture she sent to her in-laws before her engagement

Personal style at age fifteen

Porcelain Beauty
My grandmother Sayeeda Beg

Timeless Brides
My mother, a radiant bride at sixteen

...and me on my wedding day

My father Nasir Husain
Good looking, elegant.
The man who won her over

Nasir & Shahnaz
Waltzing through her life with her support and her guide

The Tehran days

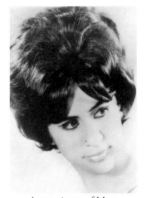

Beach beauties Mum & Me....

A rare picture of Mum
with short hair

....and growing up together

Fun & frolic
at the
Caspian
Sea

Mum on her consultation table

Where history was made...
the first salon

The glamorous professional

Motherhood

Holding me in her arms...and sixteen years later, with my brother Sameer

Mum and Sameer: Rockstars, both of them

Hollywood star
Goldie Hawn
interviewing
Mummy

The Shahnaz Husain
experience: foreign
buyers at the
herb farm

Barbara Cartland launches Shahnaz Herbals' 'Flower Power Range' in Paris

From the holiday album

Gorgeous
Grandmum:
celebrating
Zubek's
birthday

Mum blessing Sharik & Amrita on their wedding

A perfect togetherness - Tabrik & me

He was the 'wind beneath her wings'...and (inset) facing his loss

Testing her products. Applying
'Shaeyes' the hot-selling kajal

At the
Research and
Development lab.
Her eyes intently
survey the
ingredients of
her products

Fresh rose petals being added to the planetary mixer for 'Sharose'

The spectacular flagship salon in New Delhi

A blend of modernity and Ayurveda

At the 'Shahnaz Husain Signature Store' at Select Citywalk in Delhi;
Fresh herbs displayed with the product ranges here

International recognition: at President Obama's meet of outstanding world entrepreneurs

At Harvard Business School as student and speaker

Successful ladies: with Cherie Blaire & Hilary Clinton

Honoured by the nation. Receiving the
Padmashree from President Abdul Kalam

Woman Power: with Prime Minister Indira Gandhi

Worlds greatest
entrepreneur award.
Success Magazine
New York

Receiving
the APEA award

Mr Puri & Mummy
on their wedding day.
Reclaiming happiness

Mum on a merry-go-round at Covent Garden, London

Mum & Zubek — a wonderful bonding

Walking at
Hyde Park in London
— Sharik with Mum
& Mr Puri

At the centre of media attention

Barista times

Friends forever: Mum & me

The face that launched a million jars

Supporting the ladies at work–
Sharik' V.P., Shahnaz Herbals

Artist at work

Mum's favourite picture of me

Mum with Mr Puri,
walking the red carpet at Cannes

Beautiful Mum
A woman of substance

had been violated now – just when she was beginning to feel the comfort of returning to the safety of her homeland.

The authorities asked perfunctory questions and went through the motions of searching for fingerprints. My father spent sleepless nights trying to help the police work out the case but there were no breakthroughs.

The intense turmoil of a young woman faced with a startling setback even before she had started a venture she was passionate about, was painful to watch. My mother was very distressed through this phase and it was probably the only time in her life that I have seen her disillusioned. She could not believe how things had turned against her in an instant, when she was so close, her hand stretched out to touch the winning post. She now had to disengage herself from her angst and look ahead.

Eventually, there seemed little choice; we were forced to accept the stark reality that things had drastically changed. My father made the heart-breaking call to inform the landlord that we would no longer be able to take his beautiful home.

Life had come full circle. The strange ministrations of destiny led us back to the house we had stayed in as a temporary measure – M-92 in Greater Kailash I, where the ground floor had remained vacant, as though waiting for someone special. My father knew the landlord well and he managed to convince my mother that in our altered circumstances it would be a good place for her to start the salon and then move to a better area as time went on. It was an unthinkable compromise for my mother but one that she had to make. Every moment that she had spent studying and struggling, to pay for her education, it was the image of her salon in India that had inspired her to soldier on. And now she felt the years of struggle wasted; the long hours of work on her typewriter, hammering away with bandaged fingers in Tehran, violated. She was anguished and confused. This was not Westend or Diplomatic Enclave as she had dreamt; Greater Kailash then was the back of beyond, a sleepy residential enclave where the rents were low and nothing significant ever happened. Not exactly the sort of place where one would want to begin one's career.

Yet there was something wonderful about M-92, a positive energy surrounded it, a healing aura that touched all of us. My mother's exuberance returned and she set about the task of making it her own. It was as though the past and all its troubles had been swept away by a sudden flood of faith and the belief that good days were on their way.

My mother never looked back after she set foot in that house. She began setting up her salon on a threadbare budget and endless reserves of energy. If there is a debate on which is more crucial for success, money or enthusiasm, I am positive it is the latter that saves the day. Unless investments are fuelled by passion they cannot propel a business beyond a point.

The house had just two bedrooms but our ever-obliging landlord agreed to let us cover the veranda and use it as the salon. I remember my father instructing the workers and watching anxiously as the roof was built. When it was finished we had a perfectly shaped, long room large enough to accommodate the skin treatment area, the hair treatment chairs and a comfortable consultation chamber.

It was also essential to dedicate an area for making a range of Ayurvedic preparations so the front veranda facing the garden was glazed to create a room that was barely six feet by twelve feet. The room had a long, slim counter-top, a stove, a cupboard for raw materials and wooden shelves where containers bought in the wholesale market were washed and stocked, waiting to be filled. This tiny room was the beginning of the Shahnaz Herbals product range. My mother would be intently stirring a mixture, assisted by a house-help, while I made myself useful as an apprentice, filling the jars and labelling them neatly.

Decorating the salon was entirely a family project and the three of us put our brains and hands together to make my mother's dream take form. Since it was originally a veranda there were windows that opened into the house and had to be boarded up. We came up with various ideas, finally settling on a collage. Much like we were putting together a school art project, we took dozens of magazines and cut out faces of women that we pasted together to create a trendy piece of art.

The salon was beginning to come together. The next few days saw hectic activity to get the place ready for the world. Our enthusiasm and creativity and my mother's magic touch converted the veranda into a glamorous space.

It was the summer of 1970. My mother's dream had become a reality; her professional journey had begun.

The Board Goes Up

It was just a moment in time. The neighbours and passersby barely noticed the frosted-glass signage that read 'Shahnaz Husain' followed by an impressive row of qualifications. It looked much like a doctor's board with the words beauty clinic conveying the message of being a treatment centre for beauty-related skin and hair problems.

Then the doors opened and the world spilled in.

Let me take you through this place, where history was made and dreams came true, while the paint still smelt fresh. The large living room doubled as the reception area during the day. My mother's personality was reflected everywhere in it – in the family heirlooms and objets d'art she had brought back from Tehran; in the two dramatic Czech chandeliers and a royal blue Persian carpet that gave the room a warm and luxurious feel; in the lightly carved sofa dressed in Venetian tapestry with European figures lending a touch of the West.

The door on the far side led to the salon, which was painted a soft pink. The table that my mother had given my father for his birthday in Lucknow stood proudly in the consultation area. Beside it was a small, functional cabinet in dark wood where the

Shahnaz Husain range of products were neatly stored, so my mother could reach out and dispense them to her clients. What started off as personalized formulations made for individual clients, gradually grew into a range of treatment-based products. Some of the products I remember in that cupboard at the time were the classics like Shalife; Shacleanse – the cactus-and-aloe cleanser; Shafair – a remedy for pigmentation; Shagrain – our most laboriously made product; and the eternal Shatone – for hair fall. Even though the company now has a repertoire of 250 products, interestingly, these initial products have remained at the top of the company's bestseller list. Every evening my mother delighted in finding the shelves emptied out, her smile stretching across her face as she restocked them.

In one corner of the salon, in front of her desk, was a small gramophone on four legs, which played soothing music. An old, round-backed, carved chair, a hand-me-down from her grandfather's house and three comfortable chairs, made up an informal waiting area. One of the chairs was a work of ingenuity – an imposing poster of Mona Lisa framed in thick glass was the backrest of the chair. I have memories of my mother sitting at her table, surrounded by several women at once, all of them impatiently waiting their turn, chatting and interacting with her in an environment that was relaxed and pleasing. Adding another touch of glamour, forming the centrepiece of the room, was a carved metal dressing table that she had bought in France. The treatment section had just two beds and a chair for hair-care, flanked by some of the most modern gadgets of the time. The use of the latest equipment along with Ayurvedic formulations integrated the best of the future and the past.

This is where the first Shahnaz Husain skin and hair treatments began, from where the first legendary products were dispensed.

It was a simple room but one with a soul and so much love that one couldn't help but feel the warmth wrap itself around in a comforting embrace. Every inch in the room had something to say; every piece of furniture came with a blessing and a story to tell. It was a special place and will always be sacred in our memories.

The launch of Shahnaz Husain was as low-key as the frosted glass signage. The only advertisement was in the form of white cards with the words of Helena Rubinstein – '*A facial is to the face what watering is to flowers. Without it the face can never blossom and will prematurely die*' – embossed in fine gold lettering along with my mother's name and qualifications and a list of treatments available at the salon. The logo on the card said 'Woman's World', the name that was first used for the business. It was etched on a globe. The cards did not carry her picture; I don't think she had realized the power of her persona back then. She wanted to focus on her work and let it speak for itself. Those first cards that elegantly and simply reinforced her exclusive and paramedical approach to beauty and skin-care were worlds apart from the larger-than-life, glamorous image we see today.

My father came up with a novel way of distributing the cards. He drove through the neighbourhood with me by his side, supervising their delivery personally. I remember those drives vividly; I was my father's assistant, keeping track of the houses that had been done, making suggestions and generally trying to make myself useful. We made a good launch team and a highly effective one as it turned out.

The next morning my mother waited by the phone, anxious for it to ring. When it finally did she lifted the receiver instantly, her face tense with anticipation. It was a lady making enquiries.

'How much do you charge for a facial?'

'Thirty rupees,' said my mother.

There was a moment's hesitation. My mother waited anxiously.

'What time can I come in?' finally said the voice on the other side of the receiver. My mother wrote down the first appointment of her career with a flourish and then waited by the phone again. Every time it rang she answered it instantly. Her smile grew with every ring and by the end of the day her appointment diary was filled with names and contact numbers.

'Tutu,' she said, looking at my father, 'thank you so much. Let's go to the Oberoi for dinner tonight.'

It was indeed time to celebrate the first glimmer of success. The buzz had started and after that day there was never a dull moment at M-92.

The only other publicity I remember at that point was an interview by Amita Malik in *Junior Statesman* – an extremely popular journal that catered to young readers. I distinctly remember coming home from school one day and finding a camera team moving around the living room with my mother posing on the long settee and giving the first shots of her career, moving, smiling, tilting her head like a pro while the photographer clicked away, surprised at this confident young woman who responded instinctively to the lens.

'Have you modelled before, Shahnaz?' he asked her, impressed by her élan.

'No, never,' she shook her head. 'But I am enjoying myself immensely.'

When the magazine was published I remember looking at pictures of my mother and thinking: 'Wow, doesn't she look amazing?' Her hair was long and luxurious and her eyes were strong and compelling. With her perfect hour-glass figure, clad in trousers and a white cut-work top, she looked every bit as one

119

would imagine the young Shahnaz Husain to look. This was her first press coverage and it started a wave of interviews, articles and TV appearances that continue to this day. She had a magnetic persona and spoke with the energy of a crusader – no wonder public interest in her was immense.

I would say my mother was an exceptional event. In the vein of Nicholas Taleb's book, her appearance on the sedate Delhi environment of politicians and bureaucrats was like the appearance of a svelte black swan in a pond. A high-impact, low-probability event. Her story made copies of magazines fly off the racks and it was not long before innumerable journalists appeared at her door, eager to cover the new entrant on India's beauty scene.

When my mother started her salon, she did not think of hiring any staff to assist her. She considered her clients sacred and attended to each appointment personally. I remember her receiving a call in the early days of her career from a leading movie star who was visiting the city and had heard about Shahnaz Husain and her extraordinary beauty treatments. My mother politely told Sadhana that much as she would have loved her to visit the salon she had pre-booked appointments and did not have a free slot for her. A thorough professional, my mother wouldn't consider delaying or changing a standing appointment for anyone, not even a film celebrity.

Firm in her belief that 'the face was a barometer of internal health' she explained to every client the importance of internal well-being. She referred every client for a medical and pathology test and relied on it frequently to make her diagnoses. She advised her clients on their diet and lifestyle and told them of the benefits of exercise and adequate sleep. It was a holistic approach, one that accepted the different needs of the body and embraced all aspects of life and wellness.

My mother's approach to her clients was always intense and personalized. Once, a tall, attractive Bengali girl came to the salon with alopecia. Her long hair cascaded down her back to her hips but when she parted her hair at her scalp, there were coin-shaped bald patches, as smooth and hairless as the back of her hand. My mother asked her several questions and realized that the hair loss was a result of sudden shock and anxiety. The girl was the only earning member in her large family and had recently lost her job. Not only did my mother treat her free of cost, she even called one of her more influential clients for a favour and secured a job for her. She knew that what she was treating was just a symptom of the problem and the real cure lay in the resolution of her financial crisis. The young girl finally visited my mother with a box of sandesh in her hands, a beaming smile and a head full of lustrous hair.

Shahnaz Husain became famous for her remarkable cures; for the ability to deliver what she promised. She took on severe cases of acne, pigmentation, premature age lines and hair loss without hesitation. She did not even hesitate to take on challenges like burn marks. I distinctly remember her treating a young airplane-crash survivor for scarring. She often said that there was nothing more incorrect than the belief that beauty was superficial. It reached deep into the self-esteem and confidence of a woman and affected her soul and psyche as nothing else could.

My mother continued to live and breathe her work. It became her life – and still is – as her determination translated itself into a sincerity of purpose that was intense. Apart from single-handedly managing her burgeoning list of clientele, she also wrote a series of articles on beauty and was soon running several question-answer columns for leading dailies and magazines. Shahnaz Husain began to emerge as an expert on skin-care whose advice was valued as someone who had the answer to the most distressing beauty problems. The consolidation process of those early years was the key to her success. My father was also moving up the official hierarchy at the State Trade Corporation, which had grown into a very powerful organization.

Since its opening the cosy salon had grown to keep pace with its popularity. The room had been extended to accommodate more clients and two more beds had been added to it. The volume of work increased to a point where she could no longer manage alone and hired her first staff members. She was moving towards the next phase of growth, the first signs of which came when she received an unexpected business proposal.

In 1972, a lady dressed in an elegant chiffon sari walked in and introduced herself as Mrs Irani, wife of the editor of the *Statesman* in Kolkata. 'Shahnaz,' Mrs Irani began. 'I have heard so much about you. Why don't you give me your franchise for Kolkata? I promise you we will do wonders in the city.'

My mother was a little confused. She was so focused on building her immediate clientele and running the salon that she had not realized what a viable business commodity she had created.

'I will have to think about it,' she said a little possessively, not particularly happy at the thought of her clients being handled by someone else. She needed time to adjust to the change that was taking place, an adjustment she realized she had to make if she wanted to experience the expansion of her business, which was now a very real possibility.

Mrs Irani became the first-ever franchisee of Woman's World. A water-tight agreement, meant to protect the franchise and my mother's reputation in every possible way, was drafted in consultation with experts. My mother was concerned about allowing outsiders into her dream project but as she eventually realized, sharing her dream was the only way to see it grow. We flew down to Kolkata for the opening of the franchise salon at Shakespeare Sarani and a full schedule of talks with various women's groups and parties in honour of the young Shahnaz Husain. She was now a recognized figure and her reputation was growing steadily. Groups of women thronged to her eagerly, seeking advice on their skin and hair problems. The trust and implicit faith of her clients, the confidence in her that built up in them, were the cornerstones of all future growth.

Within a year of the opening of the first franchise salon it became clear that the name 'Woman's World' was completely eclipsed by its creator, Shahnaz Husain. Clients referred to it as 'Shahnaz's salon' and the products were known as 'Shahnaz Husain's products'. It was obvious that the name needed to be changed officially. Though quite young at the time, I was in favour of going with just 'Shahnaz Husain' but since my mother was keen on portraying the natural concept of her products she finally settled for 'Shahnaz Herbals', a company completely and unquestionably associated with its creator.

The Beauty Academy also became an integral part of the franchise system and the process of growth. The first classes were taken in the garage, which was converted into a lecture hall, while a section of the salon was used for practical classes. Within a few years the necessity for a much larger school area made my mother move the academy to an apartment close by. Apart from the regular students, every franchisee was also trained thoroughly at the centre. Over the years, every student who left the school proved to be an ambassador of the Shahnaz Herbals brand. The expansion process came as links of a chain; often these links were students who would go on to take a franchise. The school was also rapidly franchised along with the salons, creating a web of concentric circles of dedicated business partners.

Feeling the need to use her favourable position to empower those who were disadvantaged, my mother started 'Shamute', a philanthropic centre for training those with hearing disabilities. It was inaugurated by President Giani Zail Singh. Recently, Shahnaz Herbals started a programme for training the visually handicapped as well. It is said that Nature always compensates the disadvantaged; while those who are unable to hear have very strong concentration, those who are unable to see have an acutely developed sense of touch. Over the years the training centres for the handicapped have reached out to innumerable girls to make them economically independent and confident. I am happy to say some of these students are gainfully employed at our centres.

The year was 1978. Shahnaz Herbals was forging ahead. The rising demand for the product range and my mother's drive to take Ayurveda to the next level necessitated having a professional facility. I remember my father driving us down on a hot summer day to the upcoming Okhla Industrial Area where small sheds were being auctioned off to entrepreneurs. Acquiring her first factory and production centre was a landmark in my mother's career. We stood peering through the dusty glass into the five-hundred square metre hall that seemed large enough to contain her dreams for the moment.

The inception of the unit meant that the profile of activities would change. It was no longer about handling an exclusive salon. The setting up of the factory involved government procedures, identifying talented Ayurvedic chemists and engaging workers. My father stepped in at this point and was active in establishing every aspect of the first production unit. Though a small unit it marked the point where a level of professionalism came into the manufacturing of the products. It was the beginning of the product becoming a serious commercial proposition. It was also a turning point in the long history of Ayurvedic skin care. It was perhaps its first stepping out into the world as a viable therapeutic alternative, in the hands of a mentor who would not stop at anything to elevate it to where it deserved to be.

Throughout my mother's journey to success and fame, my father stood by her side, supporting her in her vulnerable moments, grounding her when the rush of triumph threatened to cloud her vision. He was her stabilizing factor. In the years that followed, she found she needed him more each day for his calm and gentle presence, his experience and maturity. He was her business advisor; she trusted his advice above everyone else's and never made a decision without consulting him. While she was strong and energetic, he exuded a charm and softness that was immensely appealing.

Together, my parents became a popular couple on the social circuit in Delhi; both good-looking people, young and self-confident, each in their own style. They led a hectic social life but what they enjoyed most was the company of a few close friends.

I remember my father playing chess with a dear friend, Iqbal Marwah, the head of British Airways in Delhi, while my mother chatted late into the night with her closest friends, Maharani Padmini of Jaipur, an elegant royal; Najma Bilgrami, a highly intelligent, green-eyed beauty who was featured on the cover of the French *Vogue*; and Zainub Chauhan, the dynamic Parle whiz kid, the brains behind Limca and many of her company's successes. They made an eclectic group bonded by a common strain; they were all women of substance.

Around this time my grandfather decided to accept a position offered to him in Delhi as chairman of the Law Commission. His younger brother, Hamidullah Beg, had been appointed Chief Justice of India and had moved to the capital as well. Since his wife had chosen to remain in Lucknow, my mother often took on the role of an elegant hostess for her uncle. Over the years several of my father's brothers and sisters shifted to Delhi. Finally Abba gave in and agreed to relocate himself to the city where his children lived. My parents were extremely happy to have their families in the same city. If perfection was an attainable concept, life had skilfully worked itself to that seemingly impossible point.

My Mother's Baby

The soft pink salon exuded a certain aura in the evenings; the calm and contented feel of a place that had seen a good day's work. I walked in, inhaling the usual whiff of roses and aromatic lotions that lingered in the air and looked at my mother sitting at her consultation table wearing an expression that I found hard to define. It was an evening ritual we both enjoyed. I would sit up on one of the facial beds dangling my legs and we would chat about the day's happenings.

'Don't you feel lonely, Nelofar, being an only child? It's not been fair on you,' she said suddenly that day, sitting back in her chair.

'Oh no, Mum. I am fine. Papa and you have been like friends to me,' I said dismissively.

'Well, what if I tell you that you may not be an only child for long?'

I looked up, confused, the glass of cold coffee almost slipping through my fingers. 'Are you going to have a baby, Mum?' I asked in shock.

She smiled and I went over and hugged her. 'Oh Mum, I am so happy. I am so happy!' I kept repeating in disbelief.

I was an only child for the first sixteen years of my life and though my relationship with my parents was close and loving, I did, in fact, often feel lonely, especially when I saw my friends with their siblings. However, by the time I joined Lady Sri Ram College, I had accepted the situation as I watched my mother put all her energies into building her career. I didn't expect my parents to have another child. But now, having achieved the success she had been searching for, she had decided to revisit motherhood; it had bothered her that she had only one child, more so since my father had wanted a second one for many years.

With the news of her pregnancy, our roles changed drastically. I started mothering her, supervising her diet and making sure she took care of herself. 'Have you had your glass of milk today?' was something that *I* asked her now.

Caught up in the whirlwind of work, Mum rarely remembered that she was pregnant, meeting her clients and going through packed working days. She went straight from her consultation table to Holy Family Hospital.

I remember her expression as she lay propped up in bed, looking restless and impatient; this was not a situation she was comfortable with.

'I didn't need to be admitted yet,' she protested. 'It is a false alarm; I can't sit here when I am feeling perfectly well.' With that, she got out of bed and changed out of the hospital robes.

'Shunno, you can't do that. The doctor is on her way,' said my father in shock.

'Don't worry, Tutu. Just look at me. Do I look as if I am going into labour?' My mother walked out of the hospital with an alarmed nursing staff helplessly chasing her. My anxious father drove her home, protesting the entire way.

'All I want to do is finish a little pending work and get back to the hospital in good time,' she insisted.

When we reached home, the phone was ringing persistently. It was the hospital. 'Please bring her back immediately,' said a frantic junior doctor. But my mother had stepped into her haven and was sitting back in her consultation chair, relaxed and at peace. I remember looking at her and thinking, 'Mummy has become a workaholic, this is not work for her now, it is something more. It's a *junoon*.' She worked there all day. The next morning she woke up in pain and this time just to ensure that she did not slip away again, it was straight to the labour room.

My father and I paced the musty grey corridors of Holy Family Hospital nervously, both of us tense and praying under our breaths. After an agonizingly long wait, Dr Bhandari appeared with a smile on her face. 'It is a boy. In fact, he is a twelve-pound gentleman,' she beamed.

My father grinned from ear to ear as a nurse emerged with my baby brother, still soiled, on his way to his first wash.

A while later my mother was wheeled to her room, looking relieved and composed. She looked calm and wore the serene expression that descends on the face of a woman who has just gifted the world with life.

We all stayed together, spending the next few nights in the hospital room, enjoying every moment of the birth of my brother; it was the four of us now and it felt so good.

When it was time to give my brother a name, there was no hesitation or confusion. My mother had chosen my brother's name when she was seventeen. Her friend Gomti Vyas had named her son Sameer. 'When I have a son that is what I will name him,' she had said and all these years later she hadn't changed her mind.

My father liked the name as well; it rhymed well with his: Syed Sameer Husain, son of Syed Nasir Husain sounded perfect.

In the months and years that followed I became much more than a sister to Sameer. I took care of him – from preparing his milk bottles to changing him and spending hours of complete joy playing with my new toy. I would wheel him in his pram all over the city, often assisted by my closest friends, Tina and Neeru, who were almost equally excited at the little marvel. On one of my shopping sprees I was asked: 'Is that your baby?'

'No,' I replied, a little shocked, 'he's my mother's.'

I remember complaining to my mother later, 'Mum, can you keep your baby with yourself, please? All the boys think I am married; worse still, they think I am a mother!'

My baby brother's birth was an enjoyable event at my college, LSR. When he came with his maid to pick me up, wearing his rompers and a little cap, his rosy cheeks, bulging temptingly, were constantly pinched. He was by far the most popular boy to have ever waited outside LSR and the denim-clad, cologne-doused bikers who stood outside, watched in envy as Sameer was cooed over and cuddled by all the girls. He was the darling of the college, a community baby brother.

The years between Sameer's birth and my marriage were easy for my mother. Her friends often joked that she had timed her second child carefully so that her daughter would be old enough to bring him up. Indeed, I was Sameer's second mother; he even called me Chhoti Mummy when he felt extra affectionate. In one of my wedding pictures he is seen sitting on my lap with his arms wrapped around me and from his expression it is clear that he, more than anyone else, did not want me to leave home.

Once I got married I think there was a vacuum in Sameer's life and – just as I had once been – he was on his own too. My mother's path to stardom involved travelling frequently and her work life came into conflict with her motherhood. She adored her son and hated leaving him but taking him along was not an option because he had school to attend. There were commitments that could not be avoided; award ceremonies, salon openings and conferences dotted her travel schedule. Somehow her presence at each of them seemed essential to her growth

When she arrived in Goa, for the opening of the Shahnaz Herbals salon there, her franchisee was shocked to find her being carried down the plane's stairway on a stretcher. She had high fever. After taking some strong medication she faced the crowd that had collected to meet her with a smile. Respecting commitments she had made was essential to her and dedication meant that promises had to be kept.

Even though my father found it difficult to cope with my mother's travels and the pressures that came with his job, he always managed to accompany her. She felt incomplete without him. I think her need to have him by her side was as much the result of her traditional upbringing as her dependence on him for business transactions. His ability to negotiate and tackle buyers at trade fairs and business conferences made him indispensable to the growth of Shahnaz Herbals.

My mother was back at her desk a few weeks after she delivered Sameer. The concept of working from home gave her the freedom of slipping out of the room and being with her baby whenever she could. Years later, when her own business expanded, she encouraged the work-from-home concept for women with young children.

Her bond with Sameer was intense; she tried her best to do justice to her role as a mother even as her career graph was moving beyond her control. The compulsions of success, of commitments and expectations, drove her to move ahead. A restlessness after every achieved goal became the impulse to raise the bar further. The winning post was constantly moving ahead.

Sameer was now three years old. My mother had achieved fame by any benchmark, yet once again she was restless. She was convinced from the persistent letters she got that hair loss was easily the most distressing and unresolved issue for men. She started communicating with some leading specialists and finally tied up with Dr Barnett, a world-class specialist in hair transplants in New York. My father was supportive and offered to stay back with young Sameer. 'Why don't you and Nelofar go together,' he said. 'It may be useful for her to learn with you as well.'

We took the flight to New York, with tremendous excitement, like two young friends going on a vacation together. It was perhaps the most bonding time of our lives. I was nineteen and she was in her thirties. However we were so much in awe of the Big Apple that we barely stepped out except to Dr Barnett's clinic. I realized how boring my effervescent mother could be when my father was not around. She declined every invitation, every exciting evening plan I made; she even refused an invitation to dinner with Dr Barnett's family, saying, 'Not without Papa.'

My mother was however disappointed by the intrusive procedure of hair transplants and did not feel that anyone should go through such pain and risk to reverse the course of nature. Today the Shahnaz Herbals treatment for hair-fall uses potent herbs to restore hair revival.

The excitement and speculation in media circles continued to grow and so did her fame. She was working toward bringing

India's ancient heritage to centre-stage; to move it from where it lay, languishing on grandma's shelves, to the glistening shelves of Harrods and Selfridges.

With her image firmly implanted in people's minds, her persona became the product in the years to come. She *was* Shahnaz Herbals; she was the solution to everybody's skin problem. Her face on each jar became the seal of confidence that customers reached out for. However it is important to point out that she did not merely bank on the mystique of her personality. The product was her mainstay and giving each customer the satisfaction of receiving a cure for their problem at Shahnaz Herbals was her greatest concern. The quality of the products and their efficacy was her long-term goal. 'People will buy your product once for the name but they will use it for life only if they find it effective.'

My mother had a host of celebrity clients and admirers but none as special as Mrs Indira Gandhi. At the time, my mother was constantly quizzed about whether she was responsible for the Prime Minister's perfect porcelain skin. Today, with so much time gone by, one can come out and say, indeed she was. It was at a fairly early stage in her career that she received a phone call from the Prime Minister's secretary one day. She took the call with a keen sense of anticipation.

'Madam would like you to come over to see her at the house,' said the voice.

On the appointed day my mother excitedly took a select range of her products for Mrs Gandhi. Soon she became a regular at the Prime Minister's home. She often shared a soup with her, adding a dash of the trademark Shahnaz Husain pizzazz to their conversations, which I think the Prime Minister quite enjoyed after a hard day's work.

I remember her coming back from one of her meetings with Mrs Gandhi looking a trifle worried: 'I told her a joke and I am not sure if it was the correct thing to do.'

'What was the joke?' I asked.

'A donkey kicks his owner's mother-in-law and she dies. The next day there is a queue outside his house to buy the donkey.'

I looked at her in shock. 'You told her *that* joke?'

My mother nodded uneasily.

'Did she laugh?' I asked.

'Yes, she did.'

'Well, if she laughed I guess it's fine.'

On another of my mother's visits to her residence, Mrs Gandhi pulled out a bottle of a French moisturizer and showed it to my mother. 'A friend of mine brought me this and I find it really good but I am sure you can make a better Ayurvedic version of it.'

My mother promised her that she would do her best and brought back the bottle to analyse its ingredients. After extensive research and experimentation, she put together her own formulation of herbs and oils, which resulted in the creation of Shamoist. When my mother gave a bottle of the freshly made product to the Prime Minister she said she would try it out and give her some feedback. My mother remained concerned but on her next visit a beaming Mrs Gandhi said, 'Shahnaz, I will not have to get a moisturizer from abroad it seems.'

My mother was extremely encouraged by this, coming as it did from a lady she admired so much. Years later, Shamoist retains its position as one of the bestselling products in the Shahnaz Herbals' range. Those who use it today are unaware of the interesting bit of history behind it; that it was made especially for our Prime Minister of the time and derived from a sample given personally by her.

Mrs Gandhi recognized my mother's natural charisma – her ability to draw people to herself – and at one point she was keen for her to join the Congress. She invited my mother to a conference at the convention hall of the Ashoka Hotel to get a feel of things. My mother did attend the conference, but clearly she was not at ease in political circles. Besides, my father did not approve of the idea at all. 'You are in business,' he told her. 'The moment you get into active politics you will start worrying about the outcome of every election and it will finally affect your work.'

Over the years I have seen innumerable politicians across party lines come to my mother for a pre-election make-over. I can say with conviction that there is no political party that has not been touched by Shahnaz Herbals. At the salons, we are used to political stars who come in for a last-minute touch-up – for that extra freshness before facing the public. And once the election campaign ends there is an even larger rush of politicians with unbelievably tanned complexions who can't wait to get rid of the sunburn on their skins.

I have come to the conclusion that the desire to look good is so embedded in our being that there is no one who does not explore the possibility of trying to look more appealing.

One afternoon, on a particularly busy day at the office, my intercom rang. It was my mother. 'Would you like to meet Phoolan Devi?' she asked. 'She is coming down for a personal consultation with me.'

I was surprised then but not half as much as when I decided to accompany one of our consultants who was visiting India's most lively representative in Parliament. A complete rustic, with a son-of-the-soil appeal and a natural sense of humour, he pointed at his face: '*Kucch chehre ke liye deejiye na.*' I gave him a jar of our gold cream, which he was very pleased with. Then, looking at the bottle of hair tonic I showed him next, he remarked that it was like 'fertilizer' for his hair and laughed aloud.

As I left the minister's residence, walking past his black-cat security, I thought: We are all born to desire youthful looks. We seek them, as we seek immortality; preserving and holding on to the present is intrinsic to human nature.

Although my mother chose to stay away from a career in politics, her potential and work was recognized by every successive government. She was invited to be a part of trade delegations and international women's conferences. When Prime Minister Atal Behari Vajpayee visited China as a state guest, my mother was part of the accompanying business team. Her stature as a woman achiever from the most unlikely background brought her unqualified admiration and respect, well described by Zubek, my younger son: 'She is a perfect example of integrationist India; she was born to a Muslim family, she was educated in a convent school and spent her life promoting a Vedic system of medicine.' Her traditional lineage and her ability to overcome the pressures of conforming to its demands, combined with her crusade for Ayurveda, has made her an Indian success worthy of pride.

Having made an indelible mark in the Indian cosmetics industry, she was now keenly eyeing her next conquest.

The West had yet to be won and it was not going to be an easy task.

How the West Was Won

We pushed at the heavy revolving doors of Selfridges & Co. in London and entered its swish interiors, inhaling a heady cocktail of the world's most exquisite perfumes being sprayed onto the proffered wrists of willing shoppers.

'Would you like to try this new floral fragrance by Dior?'

I offered my wrist and smelt it thoughtfully. Walking through the cosmetics section, I realized that with the exception of one Japanese brand, Europe and the United States dominated the perfume and cosmetics market completely. It was not always about the best product here but about the best marketing; it was about the deep pockets that could buy hours of television time and spend millions on packaging and advertising to create the sort of glitz and glamour that defined these super-brands.

It was a daunting proposition, yet my mother's eyes surveyed the arena like a player waiting for the games to begin. This was where she wanted Shahnaz Herbals to be placed – sold by gorgeous salesgirls in the perfectly lit aisles of leading international stores and displayed alongside the world's finest brands that promised eternal youth. Here, nothing happened by chance. Nothing even remotely close to the accidental growth of Shahnaz Herbals was possible here.

The opportunity finally came in 1980 when the Festival of India was being organized in London. Selfridges was the Indian government's chosen retail partner, offering a platform to promote Indian products and arts and Shahnaz Herbals was selected to be featured in the display of Indian products. My mother knew that this was the best opening she could ever get.

Although it was only for two weeks, my mother was determined that the presence of her product in the store would not go unnoticed. She was extremely confident of her product line but the simplicity of the packaging worried her. The commercial appeal of the Shahnaz Herbals range was going to be tested in what was the toughest market in the world for skin- and hair-care and my mother was concerned that the jars did not look sleek enough.

My parents met several designers to create a container that looked chic yet ethnic; something that would truly represent the timeless appeal of Ayurveda. There was very little time and nothing seemed good enough to stand up to the best in the world.

After many hours of experimentation it was my father who zeroed in on a small clay-pot with hand-painted flowers and leaves. The process of sealing the jar took all the ingenuity in the world but finally it became an exquisite container that looked good sitting on a dressing-table.

I watched my parents sitting in the living room, the centre table strewn with designs, mock-ups and containers, sipping tea and collaborating on ideas late into the night. Clearly their dreams were merging. I always think of that moment in their marriage as the time when they achieved perfect harmony. At the cost of sounding poetic, they were like two instruments creating an orchestra called Shahnaz Herbals. Their aspirations had become similar. Their passions had found a meeting ground and from this bond a wellspring of thoughts and ideas was emerging. Their

NELOFAR CURRIMBHOY

commonality of purpose was creating a support system for my mother. It seemed as though she was fourteen again and my father was doing her math homework. She dared. He shook his head. She ruffled his hair. He blew perfect rings of smoke from his cigarette. They laughed and I smiled watching my parents at work together.

When they flew together to London they were both equally excited for Shahnaz Herbals. My mother walked into Selfridges elated with the knowledge that she would actually be selling her products at the store. A large area on the fourth floor had been demarcated for the Festival of India. Soon it began to resemble the Cottage Industries Emporium in New Delhi. Counters displaying carpets, handicrafts, silk stoles and jewellery filled the space and the aroma of incense sticks lingered in the air. On one side, was a large stall for Shahnaz Herbals where my mother was to display her products and meet clients.

On the opening day there was an energy in the air. The announcement systems of the store were urging customers to visit the fourth floor to view India's finest products. When Prime Minister Indira Gandhi walked in to inaugurate the exhibition, there was a flutter of excitement as she stopped at the Shahnaz Herbals counter and smiled at my mother saying she was glad to see that her products were being represented at the show.

For the next two weeks my mother stood in front of the stall looking stunning in ethnic clothes, every inch the 'beauty diva from India', as the announcements in the store introduced her. She educated customers on the benefits of Ayurveda, taking care to ensure that they understood the significance of what they were buying and how it was different from the Western concept of cosmetics. The response was overwhelming and before long the shelves started to empty and the reserve stocks began to dwindle. My father looked on with pride as the clay-pot container he had created moved briskly off the shelves. People from various countries queued up in front of the counter waiting for the Ayurvedic expert to address their problems and carried away the products as though they were sacred offerings from an ancient land.

'Shahnaz,' said a deep, throaty voice. My mother turned around to face a glamorous woman with beaded braids and a dramatic presence.

'Hi, Shahnaz. I am Maizie Williams. Are you the lady from India with the Ayurvedic cures?' Several celebrities visited the festival and among them was Maizie Williams of Boney M. She had a persistent rash that had proved untreatable for some time now and had got worse with the heavy makeup that was used to cover it up for shows. My mother studied her skin through a magnifying glass and gave her Shaclove, Shaderm and Shabase. 'Try these out, Maizie, I'm quite sure your skin will look perfect very soon,' she said confidently.

Maizie returned two days later with blemish-free skin. 'Shahnaz, I am completely convinced by Ayurveda,' she said. 'I want to help promote your range and more than that, I want to tell people to stay away from chemicals.'

Maizie Williams travelled to India a few months later on my mother's invitation with members of the Boney M group to endorse Shahnaz Herbals and then followed it up with a show in Munich to introduce my mother and the Shahnaz Herbals range there. She did it purely because she was impressed with the results of the products.

Marketing experts and buyers from Selfridges often scaled the Festival floors to assess the sales potential of the displayed products; clearly the Shahnaz Herbal range was a notable success. One day as she stood at the counter, the sharp sound of heels behind her made my mother turn around. A lady with striking turquoise eyes walked up to her.

'Ms Husain,' she said extending her hand. 'I am Mary Brogan. I manage the cosmetics department at Selfridges. I have been hearing reports about your phenomenal sales and I must say the response has been very encouraging.'

'Thank you, Mary,' my mother replied, clearly pleased. 'What I am selling here is unlike any other cosmetic range in the market. I am selling a five-thousand-year-old civilization in a jar.'

Mary Brogan looked suitably impressed, if a bit confused. The next day we were invited to have tea with her in her office. 'It's not my decision, Shahnaz,' she began. 'It's the customers who have decided that they want you here.' She asked us to follow her as she walked through the store towards one of the best spots on the ground floor. 'What do you think of this space?' she said.

'It's a very good space and I am sure we will be able to do wonders here,' my mother replied, smiling.

The presence of the Shahnaz Herbals range at Selfridges gave it a credibility that was unmatched and with it came immediate access to the global cosmetics market.

A few days later, my mother pushed open the revolving doors of Selfridges and headed straight for the newly set up Shahnaz Herbals counter. She stood below a large blow-up of her picture and smiled. She was in the arena and the game was on.

Six months after it was placed at Selfridges, a nine feet long show window at Galeries Lafayette announced the arrival of Shahnaz Herbals in Paris. Sebu in Japan, La Rinascente in Milan were next. Finally, the company earned a space on the shelves of Harrods, the undisputed Mecca of international stores. Its presence in leading international chains became a catalyst to growth and

141

the exports of the company began to increase exponentially. In the years to come Shahnaz Herbals started making inroads into unexpected markets. The sales from erstwhile Yugoslavia grew to unparalleled levels and finally a production unit in the town of Tuzla was started. Japan was another surprise, being a market with perhaps the most stringent standards, it gradually became the biggest importer of the product range. The interaction with international buyers, their exacting demands and standards, were the refining ground for Shahnaz Herbals; often we created complete product ranges for particular markets. Shahnaz Herbals' emergence in the world market required extensive travel to trade fairs, promotion trips and business meetings. My mother was personally present at every launch to promote her products. She gave innumerable media interviews wherever she went and put the strength of her persona behind every venture.

The United Arab Emirates flight made a smooth landing at the Dubai airport while my mother was still hurriedly scribbling prescriptions for a row of eager airhostesses. Her secretary was handing out packets of products to the crew and some enthusiastic co-passengers who had decided to join the instantly created fan club. Dubai was the natural place to start Shahnaz Herbals' first major salon in the Middle East. For days ahead of my mother's arrival her American franchisee, Shelly Baruch, had created immense interest in the media. There were television cameras and mikes and the sound of journalists clicking pictures, as my parents walked out of security. 'Shahnaz!' said Shelly her arms thrown wide, 'welcome to Dubai.'

When my parents got into the long stretch limousine that slid on to the city's immaculate highway, Shelly looked in the rear-view mirror and saw the media van following them. 'I am sorry to take you straight to the inauguration but quite a crowd has built up and it seems they are getting impatient to see you.' And then with a broad smile, she revealed, 'We have a real surprise for you.'

As the car drew closer to the venue my parents could hear the sound of several helicopters overhead and soon it seemed that one of them was flying right over their car. My mother looked out of the window, surprised to see leaflets flying in the air announcing her arrival. Even by her larger-than-life standards this was incredible! She laughed with delight, seeing the sky above filled with kite-like objects with her picture smiling down at her. Having lived in the Middle East for many years Shelly had a fair idea of the flamboyant methods that worked in a city where life was viewed as if through a magnifying glass. Everything was opulent, dramatic and in excess here. My mother was at ease in an environment that seemed in sync with her persona. At the end of four hours, every street corner of the city was filled with pamphlets announcing the arrival of the 'Diva from India' and they were read by everybody – from men going to office, to construction workers, to the young girls with hopes of meeting Shahnaz Husain.

Yet, in all the adulation and success my mother missed Sameer, spending hours on the telephone every day trying to compensate for her absence by sending her voice to him across the miles. I did my best to be a substitute mother to Sameer while he waited patiently for our parents to return from their many long business trips but his attachment to Mummy was so strong that the strain of separation clearly showed on his face. He had all his illnesses in her absence – high fevers, the mumps, chicken pox – every childhood ailment seemed to appear when she was out of town with my father. I remember entering the bathroom one day and finding my husband standing under the shower with Sameer clutched in his arms, both of them clothed and completely drenched. Sameer had dengue and his fever had spiked suddenly bringing on a convulsion and a shower, it seemed, was the quickest way to stop his rigours. Through her trips my mother would remain anxious to find out how Sameer was doing and as much as I assured her that she should not worry, she was tormented till she returned.

When she was home, my mother was an enthusiastic parent, much like she had been in our days in Lucknow, trying to inject fun into the everyday. I remember us going for a drive to India Gate in our dressing-gowns one night, where we spotted a fancily done-up tonga with a beautiful white horse at its head. 'Let's take a ride on it,' she said impulsively. On enquiring we found out that it was a private transport and that it belonged to a family from old Delhi enjoying a night picnic on the lawns. 'Please ask them if we can take a quick ride,' she pleaded with my father. Moments later, we had all piled onto the tonga. Sameer sat in my mother's lap, the two of them wearing matching expressions of glee as the horse trotted under the starry skies.

No woman has ever achieved spiralling success without paying a price and my mother struggled to balance the demands of her career and the needs of her child. A child she loved and always will.

A Woman to Reckon With

London has always been much more than a vacation spot for my family. Over time it has become an extension of home with a company office from where a large part of the exports are handled. The shopping, the movies, the endless expansive greens of Hyde Park have a quality that is simply unmatched by any city in the world and for years we have returned there to rest for a while in the summers.

It is a city where we have had some wonderful times except for one incident that has stayed with me. It was in the summer of 1976 when the city was experiencing a particularly hot season. The British were showing their intolerance for the searing heat by dressing down. At first it was embarrassing to see so many scantily clad men and women but soon we got used to being the only fully clothed people on the scorching streets of the city.

We were walking down Oxford Street, overflowing with crowds celebrating the unusually sunny weather. The rows of stores we passed were inviting not only for their promise of great shopping but also as a getaway from the heat. Mummy and I enjoyed our short spells of freedom to shop in our all-girls group of two and we had parted from my father, promising to meet up with him for lunch. Wading through the thick crowds at Selfridges, we noticed a T-shirt printing machine. Colourful shirts with personalized messages were on display and seemed like a good gift to take back home. We picked a few styles and sizes and stood in the queue.

When it was our turn, the operator, a boy in his teens, looked right past us to the man behind and asked him to move ahead. My mother's eyes flashed in anger as she found herself pushed back. I knew for sure she would not tolerate being humiliated so blatantly but even I did not realize the extent to which she would go.

'It is my turn,' she said stiffly.

'No, it's not,' said the youngster, grinning unashamedly. He had placed his chosen customer's T-shirt on the printing table and was about to lower the heavy hot press unit that would paste a vinyl sticker onto the fabric. To my utter shock, my mother placed her hand on the shirt and said, 'You can either let me have my turn or you will have to bring that iron down on my hand.'

The smile slowly disappeared from the operator's face and was replaced by an expression of pure astonishment. In the silence that followed he glared at my mother, who stared right back at him and then he finally said, 'Let me have your shirts.'

I sighed with relief.

Later that day when we met my father, my mother proudly told him of her heroism. He was quite shaken and for several days after he avoided letting his daredevil wife venture out alone. I doubt the family and friends who wore those T-shirts ever realized the danger and daring that had gone into the process of acquiring them.

London remains a special part of my mother's life and other than this one incident we've always had the best of times in the city. Once, years later, when I was vacationing with her in London she spotted a traditional English merry-go-round with brightly painted horses. 'Come on, Nelofar,' she said. 'Let's take a ride on it.' Her spirits lit up and her eyes shone like a child's, as we climbed onto the colourful wooden stallions. She insisted on re-rounds till my head started to spin. But my mother was living her life like a beautiful fairy-tale, where make-believe and real life kept merging.

The merry-go-round at Covent Garden became such a fun spot for her that one day, when we were about to leave London, I was shocked to find her negotiating its price with the owner. 'What? Are you serious, Ma'am? Are you sure you want to take it all the way to India?' he asked incredulously.

'Come on, Mum,' I dragged her away. 'I promise I will get one made for you in India.'

There is definitely a child – a very hyperactive one – who lives in my mother. It gives her that special spirit that makes her eyes shine and her skin glow and fills her with an enthusiasm that others find difficult to keep pace with. In fact, I have made a special 'Mummy corner' in my house where I keep all her plaques and gifts. One of my favourites is a musical merry-go-round.

Over the years my parents got to know some wonderful people in London. An evening in London that I will always remember was an invitation to dinner from one of my father's friends at his home at Hounslow. 'Come along, Nasir,' he had said. 'We have a young couple from India who will sing some ghazals.' When we arrived at the quaint English cottage we were met by the enticing aroma of home-cooked food. The guests, mostly from India, were conversing in informal groups. A handsome young man in a beige kurta with large, soulful eyes stood in a corner of the living room. There was an unmistakable aura of romance about him and being all of seventeen I couldn't help noticing him.

'Meet Jagjit,' said our host, introducing us to the young man. As my father chatted with him he asked, 'So, Jagjit, what do you do?'

'I am a ghazal singer,' he said gently and then turning to the attractive woman by his side he added, 'Meet Chitra, my wife. We are hoping to release a tape of our ghazals soon.' My father promised to look out for their music in the future and wished them the best.

Later in the evening the host announced that the upcoming singers from India would be performing soon and requested his guests to sit down. Jagjit, his fingers on a harmonium, began to sing to a small group of people who seemed mildly interested in ghazals. The rest remained around the semi-detached bar area and carried on their conversations in low voices. When Jagjit began to sing I remember his voice, fresh and resonant, rising like an inferno, amazing everybody. It rose so powerfully that at that young age I felt almost shaken by its impact. A hush fell over the bar as the guests were drawn in almost involuntarily. There was absolute silence as Jagjit Singh commanded the crowd with his voice. The walls of the small cottage seemed to reverberate with the energy released within them.

As I write these lines today my mind goes back to the morning papers that headlined his death. Yet, how can that be? A voice like his never dies; it remains, it plays in one's mind, it flies on airways, it vibrates on speakers, it echoes through young singers who want to emulate their hero, it lives in the memory of every person who ever heard Jagjit Singh and his beautiful wife Chitra sing together in their blissful days. I will always cherish that wonderful evening in London, when I heard eternity.

Today the London penthouse apartment at Portman Square, just behind Selfridges, smells of my mother's trademark tea-rose potpourri, an aroma that lingers through all her different homes. Here my mother relaxes and renews her energy away from the cacophonic demands of a business life; she goes through the reams of faxes that pour in from India during the day and sits outside on the open-air terrace with friends in the evenings, balancing work and play. In the summer, London turns into the nerve centre for international trade for the company, with rows of meetings with buyers from Europe and the U.S. lined up. During her stay in London, executives of Shahnaz Herbals routinely shuttle between Delhi and London and it often feels like just another room in our Nehru Place office. Rounds of tea are served up by a retinue of familiar staff members and the smell of home-cooked food is rarely missed.

A couple of years ago I fitted our Delhi offices with video-conferencing facilities and connected them to London. On our first video conference, Mum said she wanted to sit and share a cup of coffee with me before we began work. She insisted that I send for a mug, as did she and then we sat across the miles sipping coffee and chatting while a group of officers waited to face their boss.

London in October is crisp and pure. It returns from being a hysterical summer destination engulfed by tourists and globetrotting shoppers to an exquisitely crafted city, etched by time. A touch of winter blows in the air and 'the leaves that were green turn to brown'.

My mother was strolling down Regent Street, stopping occasionally to browse at the shop windows, when she came face to face with a tall man with a white beard. 'What a surprise,' said M.F. Husain with a smile and then his eyes narrowed as he observed my mother closely. 'I would like to paint you, Shahnaz.'

'I would love that, Husain Sahab,' she replied. 'Please let me know when.'

'I want to paint you now,' said the artist impulsively.

'I have an appointment with the cosmetics buyer of Selfridges, so can we keep it for tomorrow?' she apologized.

'Well, then you will just have to cancel your appointment. You are looking beautiful. I must paint you right away, not this evening, not tomorrow but right now,' he insisted.

My mother gave in to the great master's whimsical mood.

That afternoon, when I entered the living room at Portman Square, it was washed by the light of the fading sun. I remember her sitting very still, frozen on the fur sofa. Husain Sahab studied her face and then, lifting his long paintbrush, he started filling his canvas with rapid strokes of colour. 'You are a queen, Shahnaz; you are a queen,' he kept repeating. 'I want to bring out that special quality in you. The essence of your personality must come out in this painting.' M.F. Husain looked intently at his muse.

My mother tried not to move but it was clear that she was getting restless. 'Try not to move,' the great master smiled and then asked: 'When did you last sit still for so long, Shahnaz?' an amused smile on his face.

That moment, frozen in time in the painting, now hangs in my mother's home. It portrays my mother in a flowing kaftan looking through a scalloped window. And I can almost hear M.F. Husain's voice saying, 'Sit still, Shahnaz, I want to bring out your essence. I want you to look like a queen.'

London was also home to another very special friend, someone with whom my mother shared a warm and affectionate relationship – the famous writer of romantic novels, Barbara Cartland. The lunches at her mansion, Camfield Place in Hertfordshire, were truly memorable.

Barbara presided over these, even at ninety-five, a beautiful woman, immaculately turned out in the shade of pink she made famous, her make-up perfectly done, greeting guests and enjoying every moment of her life. She always invited a small, eclectic group of people over. Her son, Ian, would invariably try to persuade me to write fiction instead of the reams of poetry I had written. He had once got my sixty-page poem 'Eyes of the Healer' read by the well-known literary agent Darley Anderson and received a reply saying that there was no doubt that there was talent and potential in the writing but he wanted me to do a piece of fiction. I remained unconvinced. I believed that like all fine things in life, poetry had its connoisseurs. The lunches would stretch into the afternoon as the conversation around the long Oakwood table in her dining room would turn compelling.

Very few people are aware of the fact that Barbara, besides being the queen of romantic fiction, was also a wholehearted endorser of alternative medical therapies and had published several books on the subject. She often made personal appearances at Selfridges to endorse Shahnaz Herbals and urged people to use the products. Barbara Cartland flew to Paris to launch the Flower Power range at the Galeries Lafayette. She even travelled to India to personally endorse the company.

She was never anything but young; age is only a number and like her innumerable heroines, Barbara remained, in her innocence and exuberance for life, forever sixteen.

Losing My Heart

The chandeliers in the living room were dimmed to create just the right light and strains of instrumental music played in the background as my parents mingled with their guests at one of the many social evenings they had hosted for their friends. One of the invitees, Meher Chinoy, was visiting from Mumbai and had called to ask if he could bring along a friend, an ex-Stephanian. 'Sure, please do,' said my father.

On the evening of the party, Tabrik Currimbhoy stood out in the crowded room from the moment he walked in. No one introduced us, perhaps because they felt no need to since I was too young but we noticed each other for sure.

I was nineteen years old at the time and my father hated any discussion of my marriage; he just could not accept the idea of my leaving home. In the mornings he was always in a hurry to get to work and if my mother tried to broach the topic in the evening, he would say, 'I won't be able to sleep if you talk of her marriage now.' But my mother, who had got married at sixteen, felt it was high time they fulfilled their responsibility as parents and found me a suitable match.

I am not sure if I had a sense that I had met my destiny at the age of nineteen but I had. A few days later, Meher, playing Cupid, called up and casually mentioned to my father that Tabrik was keen to meet me, adding: 'I told him that you are very conservative and it was best we all go out together.'

My father agreed to the suggestion and that evening I was sitting at Bali Hi with Tabrik and some friends under the watchful gaze of my parents. Tabrik asked me for a dance and, to his utter surprise, I said, 'I only dance with my father,' without hesitation. My mother had passed on her cultural instincts to me. He was quite taken aback and, according to him, that's when he decided to marry me.

After that evening Tabrik dropped by often and finally Meher suggested that my parents allow us to meet alone. For the next two months I got to know him as well as I could in the living room of my home with Bua half hidden behind the door keeping a watchful eye and simultaneously crying at the thought of me leaving her. It was, as anyone can imagine, a particularly unromantic ambience. My upbringing was completely supervised by my mother and in some ways I feel she brought me up with the same rules that her mother had set for her.

I went to college in a car with my maid in tow. 'Bua' was all of four feet but more than made up for her slight frame with her stark blue eyes and shrill voice. She became an institution at LSR because she remained at the gate through my entire college life, guarding me against any possible predators. There was a joke amongst my friends that she could smell me out! She would be in deep sleep, yet the moment I approached the college gates she would sit up and say, 'Where are you off to?' Bua never gave up being my shadow till old age forced her to return to her home in Kanpur.

Tabrik gallantly put up with Bua as well.

The opening of the first Shahnaz Herbals salon in Mumbai a few months after I met Tabrik was also an opportunity to meet his family. The Currimbhoys were an old aristocratic family of Mumbai and had once owned sixteen textile mills. Sir Ebraheim Currimbhoy was a baronet and landmarks dedicated to the family dotted the city, like Currimbhoy Road in the business district and the Currimbhoy Courts at the Willingdon Club.

My parents and I were invited to their home at Napean Sea Road where we were received by Suraiya and Asif Currimbhoy, Tabrik's parents and their pretty daughter, Naheed. His younger brother, Tarik, was an architect and was settled in New York. He later married Nayana, a novelist who recently wrote the international bestseller *Miss Timmins's School for Girls*, while Naheed married her college sweetheart, Amit Moitra, an infotech entrepreneur. The Currimbhoy home had a low-key elegance; the mahogany furniture and old family portraits gave it a timeless feel. What struck us was the distinctly European character of the family. Suraiya Currimbhoy had studied at the Sorbonne in Paris and my father-in-law was educated at Berkeley in California. Interestingly, he and Zulfikar Ali Bhutto were room-mates at college and both of them had sworn to marry the beautiful Suraiya when they returned home to Mumbai – both had the same picture of her in photo frames placed on their tables.

It was a rivalry that was taken in good spirits and finally it was the dashing Asif's ingenuity that paid off. He offered to work as a helper on a ship and returned to India before Bhutto to propose to the beauty of Mumbai. As history played itself out, Bhutto migrated to Pakistan where he became Prime Minister while my parents-in-law made their home in Mumbai.

My mother was, I remember, at her most formal that evening, dressed in a pleated beige kaftan with her normally flowing mane tamed in a neat knot. The effort she had put into deglamourizing herself was apparent. My father was dignified and gracious as always, though still a little reluctant to be there; his perfect match for me would have been a boy from his hometown in Lucknow. But the course of events was steering us towards the proposal, which finally came from Tabrik's grandmother, Zarina Currimbhoy, an amazingly elegant lady.

Discussions about the marriage seemed to be going well until the last day of our stay in Mumbai when Tabrik and my mother-in-law-to-be came over to our hotel suite to convince my mother that I should now be allowed to go out alone with him. To their utter shock, my mother declined. She had lost her voice while coping with the uncontrollable crowds that had thronged to her for advice at the opening of the salon and she was using paper and pen to negotiate my marriage. I was in the bedroom, tucked away safely and I could hear expressions of protest from Tabrik's mother and silence from my mum as she scribbled away her answer: *No, she cannot go out of the house before marriage.*

When she finally walked in after seeing them off, she was exhausted but her face bore the look of determination that I have seen often in my life. 'It's off,' she announced. 'I will never allow you to leave the house with any man till you are married.'

The centre table in the living room was littered with the sheets of paper that she had been communicating through:

No, I am so sorry but Nelofar cannot leave the house before her marriage; No, not at all; No, not even with an escort.

I stared at the words in shock. All my life I had assumed that the strict rules of conduct that my family lived by would be relaxed when I got engaged and I would be allowed to go out with the man I was to marry. But arguing was not encouraged in my family, nor was it something I had ever been inclined towards; I was just so used to rules that I accepted this as another one to live by.

As I sat on the berth of the Delhi-bound Rajdhani I told myself, *Que sera sera. Perhaps it was just not meant to be.*

My mother was still firm on her decision. 'Imagine! He wants to go out with you,' she said, sounding quite aghast.

Suddenly, amidst the noise and bustle of the station, through the barred windows of the coupé, I saw a tall figure appear in the distance. It was Tabrik. He was smiling as he got onto the train for an instant.

'Yes, Mrs Husain,' he said, coming up to my mother. 'I will accept your daughter as this mysterious package of surprises' – his words not mine – 'that will be known to me only after marriage. I will meet her under supervision in your drawing room. I accept all your terms and would like to marry her.'

As the train moved he flashed me a quick smile – under supervision – before jumping off. My mother smiled while my father looked worried and unhappy at the thought of my impending marriage. As for me, I was thrilled to bits; this had to be love, I thought, even if I could not go with Tabrik to Nirula's for Cherry Cones.

The months leading up to my wedding were filled with shopping sprees with my very own personal designer – my mother. My father was the event manager, personally organizing every detail of the wedding that was remembered for years after as one of the most tasteful and spectacular social functions in the city.

The house on Akbar Road, which was picked as the wedding venue, was illuminated with brilliant lights, twinkling back at a starry night. Dressed in a red silk gharara with gold embroidery, my great-grandmother's tika on my forehead as a blessing, I was placed like an inanimate china doll on the red velvet cladding and bolsters on which generations of the family's brides had sat before me. My face was hidden behind a heavy veil that gave me a sense of comfort and security; I was in my own private world for a while. There were no men allowed in the area where I sat but if a lady wanted to see the bride she was escorted in and the veil was lifted and my chin tilted up a bit for a better look. There were lots of voices gushing about how lovely I looked but with years of my mother and grandmother's teachings keeping me in check, my eyes remained shut.

The beats of the drums drew closer. I knew my baraat was approaching. I peered through a gap in the curtains to steal a glimpse and saw my father hug Tabrik and then pass him his cigarette for a quick drag, smiles on both their faces; it was the first sign of the warm and enduring relationship they shared in the years that followed. It is one of my favourite memories of my wedding. My mother looked beautiful in a sequinned beige sari, every bit the young thirty-six-year-old diva rather than the bride's mother, defeating all her efforts to look the part. She moved around receiving her guests and supervising the evening with her friend, Maharani Padmini of Jaipur, who had been supportive all through and had been instrumental in the arrangements. I could hear the music and the tinkle of ghungroos and tried to imagine the dancer performing a mujra in traditional finery. The atmosphere was electric and I could feel the energy of the evening even where I sat, away from it all.

My cousin stayed with me through my banishment, missing out on being part of the celebrations. Wanting to redo my veil which had got heavy on my head I asked her to lock the door so I could take a short break from my 'showing'. Just as I stepped into the washroom, I was startled by a heavy banging on the door.

'Open the door. Mrs Gandhi is waiting to come in. Why have you girls locked the door?'

'Mrs Indira Gandhi is waiting at the door,' my cousin's panic-stricken voice echoed the urgency in the voices outside. 'Quick, come out.'

I lifted my gharara to my ankles and jumped back onto the bed. My cousin threw the veil over me and I took a deep breath to compose myself. There was a hush in the room as Mrs Gandhi entered. I felt someone lift my veil and I could sense that she was looking at me. For a fleeting moment I was extremely tempted to open my eyes. Imagine holding your face up to such an extraordinary lady and not being able to see her!

The next day at the reception at the Taj Mansingh Hotel the atmosphere was lighter – until we sat down for dinner on the long tables. My two grandfathers were seated together and soon there was tension in their voices as they took divergent positions on a point of faith. I lifted my eyes for the first time through the evening and waved to my cousin, 'Parvez Bhai,' I whispered in his ear. 'Please take Abba and Nana away from each other.'

Nothing had changed over the years. One generation later, my grandfathers were still at opposite ends of the world.

When I returned from an extended honeymoon to Europe and Africa, my mother had lost fifteen kilos. She had taken the separation badly and was so unhappy that she had stopped eating. For the first time in my life I realized how emotionally bonded she was to me. Since then I have at all times been aware of the responsibility that comes with such deep affection.

Tabrik and I moved in four houses away, into a lovely Heinz villa with a sloping red roof and every morning when Tabrik left for work I would walk down to be with my mother. When my son Sharik was born the following year, I would take him with me. He loved sitting on his grandmother's lap as she interacted with her clients, proudly introducing her grandson to them. She would give him a pen and he would gleefully scribble on the prescription papers. When I am asked about Sharik's intensity for Shahnaz Herbals I always think back and say, 'He started young.'

But as Sharik grew older and my second son Zubek was born I started spending more time with my own family and gradually, over the years, my personal life became very distinct.

I was an enthusiastic mother and bringing up the boys was my life's most fulfilling experience. I got more tetanus shots than they did, playing and revelling with them. I completely endorse women who make a personal choice to be homemakers. In urban India, while celebrating the emancipated 'working woman' I equally admire those who build their children's characters and create peaceful homes as 'working women', contributing to their families and to the stability of the next generation.

Tabrik, as I soon realized, was a very private person and was particular that the sanctity of his home was preserved, that there were no press interviews in the house and the children were kept away from public gaze. I respected his desire to bring up the boys in the manner of his family, which was very low key and private.

So it was lights out at the Currimbhoy home by 11pm, while the stars were just about beginning to light up at the Husains'.

Moving to Utopia

The year was 1985. By now the surging effect of success was being felt in every aspect of my mother's life – most noticeably in her work space. The rooms of M-92 were choked with the clientele that thronged to consult her. The attention from the press, the clients, business partners and fans was overwhelming. It became clear that my mother had outgrown her first sanctuary – the small cosy salon could no longer keep up with the demands of her career. Her larger-than-life personality seemed stifled in its environs. She was poised to take Shahnaz Herbals beyond the ordinary and for this she needed to be in a space that would do justice to that vision.

Two houses down the street was a plot of land where residential apartments were to be built. It seemed like the perfect place to expand without moving too far from the original address of the business. There was more than a little apprehension about leaving the first workspace that had brought success, fame and fortune in such abundance but it was time to grow and move ahead.

With the freedom to imagine her perfect salon, my mother sketched out her vision with the skill of an amateur artist and the heart of a professional dreamer. My parents sat with the architect, Mr Sarin, a perceptive man who understood the nuances of my mother's nebulous vision and gave it a tangible shape and form. Brick by brick, the structure rose, revealing large open spaces that gave the final edifice a sense of magnificence.

I was expecting Zubek at the time and used to walk down in the evenings to find my parents, often with Sameer, standing amidst the bricks and mortar, observing the unfinished structure with the love and passion of Michelangelo looking at his paintings.

When the doors to the flagship salon were finally thrown open in the winter of 1986, an eager clientele held its breath. There was a small celebration planned for family and close friends. I drove down with Tabrik to the new address. As I stepped out of the car, I immediately noticed the gleaming black granite plaque at the gate with large gold letters that read 'Nelofar'. I was deeply touched that my parents had named this dreamscape of aspirations after me. I stood outside and took in the red-brick exterior, my eyes brimming over with emotion.

Stepping inside the main salon area, one's eyes first fell on a spectacular marble fountain gushing water on the form of a woman in pure white marble. The spiral staircase rising behind it led to my mother's offices, decorated in emerald green and turquoise blue. There were separate, plushly appointed skin-care and hair-care sections in addition to a consultation area where the client was met by an expert. It was such a large space that quite instinctively and just to identify the different areas, one started giving them names: 'White House' – the plush living room on the personal floor; 'Hollywood' – the movie room that later became Sameer's hub; 'Tiger Room' – a sitting room with a feline theme; and of course the 'Coffee Shop', which was a personalized café with wrought iron chairs, chequered tablecloths, a hissing espresso machine and snacks. The top floor of the house was purely residential and was called the 'Dream Floor'.

Standing at the stylishly designed picture-window in amber tinted glass, in my parents' new bedroom, I looked on silently at the enchanting view of the hillock and temple that had stood beyond the simple iron grill and net window of our earliest home at W-33 and later could be glimpsed from the garden at M-92. Destiny had us on the move and yet in some ways it seemed as though we were twirling in the same space.

As he grew older, the terrace flat became Sameer's haven; essentially a bachelor pad with plush leather sofas and huge posters on the walls. My brother had a finely tuned sense of aesthetics and this was the one area of the house where my mother's personal style was missing. The room facing the terrace was converted into a personal gym leading into a music room equipped with state-of-the-art equipment. This hub of creativity would come alive in the evenings with cups of coffee and friends as audience, while Sameer played out his compositions, observing their reactions keenly from the corner of his eye. Sameer was passionate about becoming a rap singer. He was extremely focused. His versatility and talent often amazed me. He was writer, composer and singer in equal measure. As his voice resonated through the massive speakers, they propelled his music through the walls, piercing several layers of concrete to blast into the neighbours' houses. My mother was inundated by complaints from sleepless residents. But when you saw Sameer creating a tune – his eyes shut in intense concentration, singing almost as if he was layering the mike with his voice – it was impossible to ask him to tame his talent in any way.

My mother finally found a solution with some help from her architect. The music room was made sound-proof. Sameer spent many years raising his voice to a ringing crescendo while the neighbours slept peacefully.

The interiors of my mother's salons and homes are talked about and covered in international magazines but what's interesting is that they are a result of minimum planning and complete chance and randomness. Things happen here; they come together, often the look changes depending on the country she has recently visited. The terrace at M-86 was one such area of chance and whimsical – almost playful – inventiveness. Partially covered to make it weatherproof, with plunging loungers, hammocks, a billiards table, a music corner complete with a guitar and keyboard and a couple of easels with artworks in progress, the space had a relaxed feel to it.

In the evenings, my parents would often move to the terrace and my mother would light-heartedly add a brush of colour to Sameer's canvas. Sameer's affair with the arts was all-encompassing. He painted boldly – his strokes were remarkably strong and confident, as M.F. Husain once pointed out.

In the years to come the roof-top became the venue of many feisty parties with food, music and a lively dance floor. There was always a distinct, carnival-like atmosphere of unbridled revelry; an unapologetic celebration of life.

At one of the many evenings a party was in full swing – the waiters were moving around with laden trays, gingerly balancing them like trapeze artists. The music was enticing, the dance-floor an indeterminate expanding space of mirth and energy. Conversation flowed as did drinks and food. Everyone seemed to be having a great time that evening except for two people. One was a tall eighty-year-old man and the other was an eight-year-old boy, Zubek, the grandson of the hosts. Tonight they had a lot in common. They both looked bored and disinterested in the revelry around them.

As they looked at each other across the room the years between them melted. M.F. Husain waved out, a broad smile on his face and Zubek walked up to him politely.

'Are you bored, beta?' he asked.

Zubek nodded.

'So am I,' said Husain. Then plucking out the black felt pen he kept ready at all times for inspirational moments such as these, he drew a jagged outline of his famous stallion on Zubek's shirt and signed it with a flourish. In an instant Zubek's humble white T-shirt became a priceless objet d'art. Zubek looked pleased, if a little confused. I smiled as I watched India's Picasso forge a bond with my young son and display a side of him that was forever young at heart.

Those evenings in my parents' home will always be a wonderful memory. Friends, family and staff all shared in the best of what I now call the days of 'Camelot'. Some places are blessed because they see so much happiness; so much positive energy flows through their walls; so much laughter rings within them. Not many places can be fortunate enough to be home to all this and more. M-86 Greater Kailash, Part 1 was one of those charmed addresses.

On the professional front, the Shahnaz Husain flagship salon became a destination point for everyone, from movie-stars to politicians, from exporters and businessmen eager to become a part of the success, to the women seeking to buy a jar of a Shahnaz Herbals' product. The salon's environs always had a current of excitement and vitality; a rub-off of my mother's presence in the building; a spillover of her boundless energy.

The clients, far from objecting, had got quite used to the occasional flurry of activity and some, it seemed, quite enjoyed being part of the inimitable Shahnaz mystique. Amongst the clients who frequented the salon through the years were many leading movie-stars who always added a touch of glamour with their presence. There were several very confidential meetings with actors losing their hair and with some who were anxious about the early signs of time and age appearing on their million-dollar faces. These were moments when my mother met the demi-gods at their most vulnerable and their visits were always kept a close secret.

The next few years witnessed rapid expansion. I think the new environs of the company's head office propelled growth and accelerated exports to record levels. Fortunately, the neighbouring property was put up for sale and it became a natural progression to expand operations there. The extra space was utilized as offices for the burgeoning staff employed to support the Shahnaz Husain Group of Companies, as it was now called.

With such swift growth, it became imperative to have a research and development centre, where herbs could be grown and tested for their efficacy, where the focus would not be on deadlines but planning new products. After an extensive search my parents chose a farm at Dhauj, in the foothills of the Aravalli range.

The structure is a testament to my mother's sense of perfection and her intolerance of anything less. My parents had meticulously planned the layout of their herb farm before leaving for an extended business trip. On their return they were anxious to see how the construction was progressing. After driving down the bumpy roads, when they finally arrived to see the building, my mother looked at the unfinished construction in shock.

'What have you done?' she asked the contractor. 'Why is the building so close to the boundary wall?'

'Madam, because there are only farms around and there is no traffic here.'

'Please break it down immediately and take it back to the centre of the area,' she said and then left.

It took two years to build the research facility to my mother's exact specifications but when she returned to Dhauj, it was to find the structure set perfectly in the middle of the plot, as she had asked.

At the inauguration of the research centre, family, friends and staff members arrived to a traditional welcome with drums and the resident camel.

'Madam is wearing a village dress,' one of the shocked farm-hands exclaimed. Clad in a multicoloured lehenga, my mother delighted everyone with her complete harmony with the atmosphere.

'The villagers are very excited about your arrival, Madam,' the manager, Mr Kapur, informed her, without the faintest idea of what he was getting himself into. 'They all want to see you.'

'All right, Mr Kapur, please find out how many houses there are in the village.'

'Madam, there are about two hundred homes between the two villages on either side of the farm,' he said after consulting with the others.

'Send a car to the nearest sweet-shop and ask for two hundred boxes of laddoos,' she said.

'Of course, Madam,' Mr Kapur replied and returned in a short while with a car laden with neatly wrapped boxes tied with golden ribbons. 'Madam, would you like someone to distribute the boxes in the village?'

'No, Mr Kapur, I will take them to each house myself,' she said, smiling back at the shocked manager.

'But Madam, it is not safe for you. There could be a stampede. There could be a law-and-order situation,' Mr Kapur spluttered, desperately trying to dissuade his boss.

'Just inform them that I would like to visit them. I am sure they will take good care of me.'

My father was pleased with the idea as well and felt it was a nice gesture.

'Madam, the village lanes are too narrow for a car,' Mr Kapur said in a last-ditch effort to change my mother's mind.

That seemed to please her even more. 'So get a bullock-cart,' she suggested, beaming at the prospect.

Sure enough, my parents climbed onto a bullock-cart that was hastily arranged for and accompanied by some members of the company's team, went down to the nearby village. Turbaned men, women in brightly-coloured clothes carrying babies, grannies – they all collected to welcome their courteous new neighbours and the narrow lanes came alive with excitement.

Sameer and I watched as our parents went from home to home, hugging and embracing people, giving out boxes of sweets and spreading so much goodwill in the tiny hamlet that I couldn't help thinking what a charismatic political couple they would have made.

Perhaps.

Who knows what might have happened if destiny had strayed a little. But then the land of 'if' is a place we can never visit.

Goodbye Hero

'Shahnaz, I would like you to give a talk on Ayurveda to the wives of the heads of the Commonwealth states on the twenty-third of November. I think they will find it very interesting,' Mrs Gandhi said to my mother on one of her visits to the Prime Minister's residence. She had taken a personal interest in making sure the dignitaries and their wives had an enlightening visit, with opportunities to experience different aspects of Indian culture. She considered my mother the brand ambassador of Ayurveda and saw in her a woman who had done India proud.

My mother was honoured to have been personally asked to speak by the Prime Minister and for the first time in her life she did not rely on her spontaneity and prepared an informative talk on skin- and hair-care through Ayurveda. She was told by the protocol chief that the ladies were keen on meeting India's beauty diva and hearing her speak and she wanted to make sure she represented India's ancient heritage at its best.

Little did she realize that the intensity of her passion for her work would be put to its ultimate test during the conference of the heads of state of the Commonwealth countries in New Delhi.

On the morning of twenty-second November, my grandmother called.

'Papa has been ill all night,' she said. 'Can you bring a doctor and come soon?' There was an urgency in her usually calm voice that was unmistakable and my mother knew she had to hurry. With my father at the wheel, we drove at break-neck speed through the city until we finally arrived at 10 Willingdon Crescent.

'Why didn't you call me earlier, Mummy?' my mother asked, rushing into the house.

'Papa insisted that I should not disturb you while you were sleeping.'

We rushed into the room and saw my grandfather lying on his bed, his usual smile missing from his pale face.

The doctor had arrived ahead of us and seemed extremely agitated: 'He is having a massive heart attack,' he said in a panic-stricken voice. My grandfather was rushed to the nearest hospital in an ambulance, its screeching siren violating the morning silence. The medical facilities in those days were fairly basic and the benumbing listlessness that is sometimes the case with overworked hospitals seemed to add to our feeling of complete helplessness.

When the doctor came out of my grandfather's room, we looked at him anxiously, hoping for some positive news. Instead he said, 'Justice Beg's heart has been irreparably damaged. He has very little time. If there are any family members that you would like to call to be at his side you should do so right away.'

I remember thinking, 'Why is he saying that? My grandfather is still alive.' My mother was stunned. Her father was her hero, her superman. Heroes didn't die.

We went in to meet him; he looked composed and perfectly at peace. As our eyes met we tried to say our silent goodbyes to him, to convey how much he meant to us. My grandmother sat beside his bed like a frail statue, her expression stoic, her lips moving soundlessly in prayer, the pallu of her cotton sari covering her head as always. My mother and I stood on either side of him just looking at his face, absorbing his image in our minds to carry with us forever. We shared this God and loved him immensely.

The next morning, on the twenty-third of November, my grandfather's life faded away. My mother looked at my father and said, 'Tutu, Papa has gone,' in a shattered voice. It was the end of an era in her life. She was now on her own; her source of inspiration and support had left her. We returned home after a sleepless night, our energies spent. Sameer was waiting at the gate with a maid, looking tense and anxious for news. My mother hugged him and he began to sob sensing the grief in her and then she suddenly looked at her watch. It was 9am. Her heart missed a beat and she picked up the phone with unsteady hands and dialled Mrs Gandhi's residence. The Prime Minister came on the line.

'Mrs Gandhi, my father has just passed away. The conference starts in an hour, what should I do?' Her voice shook; the emotional turmoil within clearly evident.

Mrs Gandhi was silent for a while and then she said, 'Do what your father would want you to do.'

The answer left her a choice yet gave her the inspiration she needed so badly, to hold herself together and make a brave decision. Taking a deep breath, she stood up and walked to the oval mirror; the woman who looked backed at her had tired, empty eyes, her million-dollar smile trapped in the stifling grip of grief. She put on her make-up and lined her eyes and wore the brocade kaftan she had had made especially for the occasion. When she emerged from her room she was Shahnaz Husain, but within she was a grieving daughter who did not have the luxury to mourn her father's death.

'I would like to welcome the distinguished ladies present...'

The chandeliers in the banquet hall at the Ashoka Hotel sparkled; the light was blinding and uncomfortable, exposing the pain I felt. Fighting back my tears, I looked at my mother, worried, wondering at what point she would break down but she displayed nothing but the composure and devotion that she brought to her work as she addressed the guests at the event in a controlled and stoic voice.

The next day, the red brick salon was besieged by security personnel as twelve wives of the Commonwealth heads of states visited the salon to consult my mother on beauty concerns common to all women. It was the most high-powered group of ladies we have hosted. None of them got the slightest inkling of the tragedy the family was facing.

Her father would have been proud of his daughter that day; of the woman she had become.

Crossroads

M y grandmother shifted in with us at M-92 and spent most of her day reading the Urdu newspapers, silent and thoughtful. She would often play with Sameer and Sharik, or sit with me and chat about Lucknow. Zubek dropped by every morning to meet her with a bunch of leaves. Unable to arrange for flowers every morning I had convinced him that green leaves were just as pretty as flowers. She always smiled looking at his bunch and added them to a vase she kept at her bedside. Yet the loss showed on her face even though she rarely spoke of it. The purpose of her life, my grandfather, was no more and I don't think any of our efforts to bring cheer to her life ever really brightened her again. After some empty and listless years in Delhi, she returned to live in Lucknow with her son at Marble House, her first home, to which she had come as a young bride.

For my mother the months after my grandfather's death were distressful and she immersed herself in work. It became her refuge and saviour while she came to terms with the loss of her father and her hero.

The momentum that had started with the opening of Mrs Irani's first franchise salon in Kolkata, continued to build through the years and in time the Shahnaz Herbals franchise became one of the most sought-after brands – one that guaranteed instant success and returns.

My parents, Tabrik and I were at the newly opened China Garden at Om Chambers in Mumbai, where, over plates of steamed lobsters in szechwan sauce, my mother was being pursued with a very attractive offer: the creation of the largest-of-its-kind Shahnaz Herbals salon at Kemps Corner. I was thrilled at the idea of having a state-of-the-art centre in one of the most expensive commercial properties in the country. That is how I had always envisioned the company being represented in this city, the glamour and glitz capital of India and had spent time identifying the right investor and franchisee to do justice to the name. However there was a catch: he wanted this to be the only representation in the city.

'Mrs Husain,' he told my mother. 'I will be working very hard to create a place which will be the ultimate in class and style. The clients here will be the top celebrities of this city. I cannot have the same brand name being used in a small apartment. It will completely dilute the image.'

My mother had always encouraged housewives and small investors to join the franchise chain and they were an important part of her growth.

'I know you will put in several millions into the project but what about the twenty women who have invested their life savings in my name? I could never dream of betraying their faith in me,' Mum said with a conviction that was intense.

The gentleman looked surprised; given his successful reputation he could not imagine she would walk away from his offer but perhaps the twenty women who had invested in Shahnaz Husain would have.

With my mother's philosophy of encouraging and empowering women entrepreneurs, the Shahnaz Herbals franchise of salons and the product range made its presence felt in the lives of women all over the country. Its dedicated clientele was growing steadily and so was the personal popularity of its creator. Industry watchers now sat up and started taking note of the company as a potential gold-mine, speculating what direction it would take after its initial flush of success. Business consultants and experts labelled it 'the most promising possibility in a long time on the Indian business radar'. They saw in Shahnaz Herbals the potential of a multi-crore company but for that it needed to make certain vital moves and changes in its business philosophy.

The company stood centre-stage on the business map of the country creating a clamour amongst consultants, who made a beeline to meet my mother with the hope of persuading her to open the doors of her company to waiting opportunities.

'Madam, we think your company is ready to go public and that you should not miss out on this opportunity to take it to the next level. Our studies have shown that Shahnaz Herbals has the potential of becoming the largest player in the field and the timing is perfect to go public.'

I could sense my mother resisting the consultants' rapid-fire; the idea of allowing anyone access to her crown jewels was unbearable to her.

'What is the minimum percentage of shares I will have to put out in the market? Does that mean that I will have to have shareholders on the board? Will I be answerable to them? If one person were to manipulate more than a certain percentage of shares, would that give him veto powers?'

At the end of the day, the structure of a company must be in sync with its owner's nature. My mother does not like being answerable to anyone and has always enjoyed the freedom to take her company in the direction that she wants. That freedom for her is priceless.

My mother went through the exercise of meeting a battery of consultants but it was more to experience and assess her growing success and the position of Shahnaz Herbals in the market than to consider the idea of going public. Although she had convinced herself that she was open to the concept, deep inside the thought of losing even the slightest control of her precious company was anathema to her. The business philosophy of Shahnaz Herbals was also strongly influenced by my father, who was a very cautious player. He believed that consolidation was just as important as growth, perhaps even more so and that over-ambitious companies usually ended up risking and often losing everything. He understood my mother's nature better than anyone and knew that, for her, complete and total ownership was the best way to go.

The newspapers speculated for a long time whether Shahnaz Herbals would indeed go public and the buzz continued for a while until it became clear that this would not happen. An *Indian Express* report on the seventeenth of August 2000 said, 'Shahnaz Husain applies vanishing cream on initial public offer plans.' What is commendable is that Shahnaz Herbals is a zero-debt company. It has never borrowed from any bank and its investments in its growth and expansion have been completely self-generated.

The first business person to foresee the potential future of Shahnaz Herbals was Bhai Mohan Singh, the patriarch of the Ranbaxy group and a friend of my father's since our days in Tehran. This astute gentleman made my mother an offer to become a partner in a company he was launching under the name of Naturelle. My parents spent several days discussing the prospect of partnering with Ranbaxy but in the end my father suggested that they remain an independent company. My parents politely told Bhai Mohan Singh that it was too early in her career for my mother to commit herself to a partnership and wished him well in his venture.

Bhai Mohan Singh did go ahead with Naturelle but it did not make an impact on the Indian market, while Shahnaz Husain, the lone crusader, achieved unprecedented success with no investors or advertising.

How did she do it? That is a question that is constantly asked by business-watchers and aspiring entrepreneurs trying to decode the secret of Shahnaz Husain's success. What qualified her for the position of being the country's most successful businesswoman, a success that transcended wealth and many conventional parameters, a success that enveloped glamour, admiration and respect?

Having been the person closest to her and having walked the journey with her, if I were asked what the single-most important catalyst in her success is, I would quote her personal mantra: 'I don't believe in Destiny; you are what you *will* yourself to be.' This is a line she quotes and lives her life by. Her resolute disbelief in the concept of kismet, her constant struggle with it, is the very basis of her life and always will be. She completely disregards that translucent grey area we turn to at all times to absolve ourselves of any responsibility for our existence; the resignation to circumstances that are believed to be beyond our control; that in the palm of our hands or on the lines of our forehead we carry a pre-written script and nothing can change it; that life is what is given to you and you must suffer it as your destiny.

As Zubek explains, 'Every destiny has a "by destiny". That is why we show our hands to palmists – because we believe that we can *change* our destinies, if we are warned. Then how can there be just *one* destiny?'

Point taken, Zubek.

I personally feel that your destiny and your 'by destiny' move together, like two rail tracks and you move from one to the other, depending on how strong your will power and the desire to change your life is. My mother never accepted any act of destiny and remained in constant conflict with it, fighting back to change her life around and rewriting the script of her life as it unfolded.

Neither her early marriage, nor the loss of her father, nor anything that you are yet to read in the pages ahead, had any effect on her determination to walk out a winner in the game of life. My mother does not just live life, she defies it.

When East Met West

Two women at opposite ends of the world – one a modern-day Nature Czarina, the other, Ayurveda's Reigning Queen. Both self-made women who had the courage to follow their dreams and create formidable empires from scratch.

At around the same time that Shahnaz Husain was introducing the world to Ayurveda and establishing the Shahnaz Herbals range of products, another woman, halfway across the world, was setting up a small enterprise known simply as The Body Shop, with a modest range of beauty products in refillable containers.

In 2001, my mother took a flight from New Delhi to Chennai to spend the day with this very special person whom she admired and whose career she had followed closely. Anita Roddick had been watching her meteoric rise too and admired her equally. Representatives of the Body Shop chain had visited my mother several times over the years to find out more about the company.

The drive to the farm near Chennai, where she was staying, was through a sprawling landscape of lush green foliage and tall bamboo trees. As the car drove up to the porch a woman with flashes of flaming auburn in her untamed curls came out of the house.

'Hello, Shahnaz,' Anita Roddick, the founder of The Body Shop, said, stretching out her hand. 'I have waited so long for this day.'

'Hello, Anita,' my mother replied, hugging her. 'So have I.'

Despite their hectic schedules, both Anita and my mother had been very keen on meeting each other for some time now and their offices had carefully chosen a date and venue that would suit them both. As they sat down for a cup of the finest Nilgiri tea they looked at each other with mutual admiration and respect. They chatted about the remarkable similarities in their lives and business philosophies, exchanged stories about the beginnings of their businesses and the path that had brought them fame and success.

'I am so glad that you have acknowledged the great wealth of herbs in your country. As you may know, many of our ingredients are sourced from here.' Anita Roddick's farm was the base from where she operated to bring some very traditional Indian herbs into her range of products.

With so much in common, the two women spent the day chatting together. The similarity in the pattern of their careers was startling. While Anita reminisced about her first workspace – in a garage where she stored interesting ingredients – Shahnaz told her how she started making her products in a tiny veranda for individual clients. They had both started out in the seventies and had never looked back, their individual businesses expanding beyond their wildest expectations. Finally, when the sun set, my mother noticed her anxious secretary Mr Kutty trying to remind her that it was time to leave.

'The day has passed and we still have so much more to talk about. Thank you for your hospitality but if I don't leave now I will miss my flight back to Delhi,' my mother said reluctantly.

'Before you leave, let me share a secret with you, Shahnaz,' Anita smiled and opened her bag. 'Look what I have here.' It was a wand of Shahnaz Herbals' kajal. 'I have used it for years,' she giggled.

'I am so happy to see you use it,' my mother responded. 'You have chosen well.'

The two ladies, now friends, promised to meet again. Sadly, that was never to be. Though they stayed in touch, they were completely immersed in managing their empires.

Anita Roddick died of a haemorrhagic stroke in London on the tenth of September 2007 soon after giving a speech. The last time my mother had seen the vivacious lady she was walking into the sunset at her farm in Chennai with tall palm trees swaying gently behind her.

It was clear now that Shahnaz Herbals was being watched by several international players, especially those who intended to enter the Indian market. There were reports that Estée Lauder was watching the company very carefully and considered it the only serious competition they would face in India. In fact, industry reports suggested that Shahnaz Herbals was the primary focus of study of all new entrants in the cosmetics business – whether international or local – and it remains so even today.

The Estée Lauder Group had been looking at the market for a long time but they were not sure if it was ready for them. We had been getting regular feelers through consultants that they had an interest in working in some way with Shahnaz Herbals. A steady line of communication was established, which culminated in top members of their team visiting India for a meeting with my mother and inviting the family for dinner at the Imperial Hotel in Delhi. Through the evening my mother heard them out most patiently but looked unconvinced. Their thought process was clear. They wanted a tie-up with Shahnaz Herbals for the marketing of Estée Lauder in India.

Personally speaking, I felt it was a recognition of the company's position to be singled out by Estée Lauder and that an association with them was a good move since it would create a spill-over effect in the international market. However, my mother completely disagreed and felt that the tie-up was of little benefit to her. She was the trusted face of her brand and she was not willing to endorse anything that did not flow through her fingers, especially a line that was not based on Nature. Her business strategy had always been very consistent and her confidence in Ayurveda and her products had ensured that she was not affected by the size of multinational giants. The overarching Indian-ness of her career vision was obvious and when put to the final test, it was clear that it was non-negotiable.

Unaffected by the offers of international tie-ups, Shahnaz Herbals created its own path for growth. Over time, the persona of the company began to change; a metamorphosis that was neither planned nor imagined, but an organic response to the consumers' demands rather than the outcome of a well-thought-out business strategy.

My mother's vision for her company had always been to expand her chain of franchise salons and dispense her line of products through these centres, maintaining their exclusivity. She believed it was essential for a client to be seen by a trained specialist, her internal health issues handled by referring her to a general practitioner and then prescribing her a treatment programme designed in conjunction with a range of home-use products that my mother fondly called 'homework'.

This ideal situation was interrupted when murmurs that spurious products, allegedly from the Shahnaz Herbals line, were being sold in various shops all through the country.

A routine production and marketing meeting was in progress when my father entered with one of the managers.

'Look at these,' he said, placing a few jars on the table. 'Look carefully,' he added, seeing the confused look on everyone's faces.

'These are our products,' said my mother.

'They are not,' my father replied. 'They are fake and bought from the wholesale market.'

Sameer was extremely upset at what he felt was an unfair deal to the company. Since the company had no distributors and had never sold any of its products in the market, the news came as a shock to us. When we investigated, we discovered a black market that was flourishing because of non-availability from the company. The market was obviously hungry for Shahnaz Herbals and because there was an overwhelming demand the product had found its way to the stores in one guise or another.

Feeding the market through legitimate channels seemed a prerequisite to prevent counterfeits from flooding the shelves. It was time to change the company policy and appoint official distributors. The first distribution channel was established in 1989 in Mumbai, the biggest market for all retail products. The response was overwhelming and instant. Gradually, the network began to grow as distributors across the country sensed an opportunity and sent in applications to represent the company.

As the network expanded, the Shahnaz Herbals' jar broke through the confines of exclusivity and appeared on shelves all across the country. In a couple of months, sales gained unprecedented momentum. Shahnaz Herbals was an interesting example of a company that first created a market quite incidentally by remaining exclusive and then supplied an already existing demand. The Okhla factory was equipped to handle the existing franchisee chain but meeting the cascading demands of a national network was something it was not equipped for. The emergence of Noida as an industrial zone where large tracts of land were available became the next milestone in the company's growth. In 1992, the company acquired a plot to build a production facility that could meet the rapidly rising demand for Shahnaz Herbals' products. The factory was personally designed by my father who envisaged it as a sprawling low-lying structure. The earthy exterior of the factory was similar to M-86 and gave the facility a 'close to Nature' look even though the interiors were white and pristine. The front area that housed the offices and conference rooms bore the customary Shahnaz touch – the chandeliers that she had brought back from Tehran and which, for years, had lit up her first salon at M-92 were restored and given pride of place. It's a wonderful tradition my mother maintains where new and old objects lovingly bond together so there is no cut-off point, no beginning and no end, just continuity. Nothing is forgotten, nothing is abandoned, as the old and new mingle to become one.

The inauguration of the factory at Noida was a landmark, the point when Shahnaz Herbals made the switch from being a service-based enterprise to a retail- and production-based company.

My father watched as my mother scaled each successive landmark. He looked on with the joy of a man who had supported her, led her by the hand in her weaker moments and smiled as she had flown high, never letting go of his grip for a moment. He continued working with the State Trading Corporation even when her success had reached its pinnacle. Having his own work-life meant a lot to him and I think it gave them, in Kahlil Gibran's words, the perfect 'spaces in their togetherness'.

With the inception of the Noida factory the dynamics of my mother's working life changed. The company had grown into a formidable entity and she was finding it exceedingly difficult to manage the different arms of the business. She needed my father more than ever and he could sense this. It was also becoming difficult for him to manage the pressures of Shahnaz Herbals and a full-time job. On many evenings, he drove straight from his office at Connaught Place to the Noida factory. It was his baby as much as my mother's and he found it hard to detach himself from it.

In 1990, my father decided to resign from his job to give all his time to Shahnaz Herbals. On his last day at work I remember him returning home looking pensive; as though he had lost something he loved. He remained silent and thoughtful all evening but the next morning, it was endearing to see him wake up at his usual time, get into one of his perfectly cut suits, sit at his office table and start work. His personal secretary, Mr Ajmer Singh, had chosen to leave with him since he felt he could not work with anyone other than his gentle boss. At his usual office lunch hour, he got up and went to the dining table for lunch and returned precisely within an hour. He had imbibed a lifetime of the work ethos of the government and it had become a part of his being.

With his rich experience in trading at S.T.C. he took over the company's export division. It was reassuring for my mother to have my father at work along with her. Soon he took over the running of every department and became the protective guiding force of the company. His presence was all-pervasive, yet it remained enigmatic, strong and silent.

While my mother's career graph was spiralling upwards, Sameer was growing into a handsome young man, constantly chased by a bevy of girls. Slim and with an infectious charm, his passion for rap music made him very popular amongst his friends. He enjoyed dancing and was a regular at Ghungroo, the discotheque at the Maurya in Delhi. My parents worried incessantly about him. They felt it was a good idea for him to settle down, especially since both of them spent a great deal of time away from home, often for several weeks at a stretch.

It was at my cousin's wedding in Patna that Sameer, all of twenty-two, met his future wife. They were married a couple of months later at a spectacular nikah ceremony. Just like my wedding, his too, was an elegant and traditional affair, hosted on the lawns of a house in Lutyens' Delhi.

When Success Came Searching

New York City wore a haunting glow as the leaves turned to riveting shades of flame in early fall. My parents drove down to the ritzy address of *Success* magazine on Fifth Avenue where my mother was to receive the World's Greatest Woman Entrepreneur Award. With a group of directors and select invitees from the world of business looking on, the chairman of the 107-year-old iconic magazine took the mike.

'In our research to choose the World's Greatest Entrepreneur, we called upon business leaders, journalists, entrepreneurial organizations and trade offices. We looked at hundreds of candidates. We wanted entrepreneurs who not only had strong businesses but had set an example by defying fate and taking the future into their own hands. In India, we kept hearing one name over and over again: Shahnaz Husain. She is indeed a remarkable, dynamic and brilliant individual. At *Success* we are experts in entrepreneurship and I can tell you that Shahnaz Husain is the quintessential entrepreneur.'

It was amazing for the young girl from Allahabad to be sitting in New York, the city of dream merchants, among the likes of Donald Trump. Quite incredibly, in this land of emancipation, she was the first woman to receive the award in its 107-year-old history.

Throughout her career my mother has been sought out by international organizations wishing to honour her. Spain felicitated her with the Arch of Europe. This was a landmark award for the quality of the product and meant a lot in business terms. The American Biographical Institute honoured her with The Millennium Medal of Honour. This was followed by the Leonardo da Vinci Award at Oxford and the World Medal of Freedom in the US. In recognition of her international standing she was invited to the *Forbes* Global CEO Conference in Sydney in 2005. She was featured in the United Nations sponsored film, *Women of the Decade*. The list of awards and recognition is endless. It can in fact go into pages.

The persona of Shahnaz Husain was also making inroads in the international glamour world. She was invited to the Cannes film festival where she walked the red carpet. Her enigmatic personality and visual appeal also caught the eye of Hollywood and she was contacted by Mantosh Devji an American of Indian origin and the author of *Taj Mahal: A Lover's Story,* to play the role of Noorjehan in an adaptation of her book by an international film production house. There was immense speculation whether my mother would accept the offer but I was sure she would decline. It meant leaving her work for far too long and also, I think, she was restricted by the values she was brought up with.

The continued success of Shahnaz Husain has defied every established principle of advertising and marketing. Over the years she has been visited by professors from top universities like Harvard, Cambridge and McGill, among others, to try and understand her methodology, her business model and the strategies she uses. The fact that Shahnaz Herbals has never advertised and has still become a household name in a country as diverse as India has baffled business experts. I am sure that they all left conceding that Shahnaz has a highly developed business instinct and is a natural at what many spend years mastering.

My mother has always had a way of making instant, intuitive decisions that invariably turn out to be correct. Often, at meetings, when we are busy analysing figures and going over the logistics of a project, she gives her opinion in a flash. That's sheer business instinct. It is not cultivated or learnt, it's just second nature to her.

When my mother began her career in India she definitely brought to it her unique personality; the glamour of a Hollywood diva, the charisma of a rockstar, an astute business mind and thorough professionalism. In addition, she had a diligently acquired education and a passion for her cause. It was a stunning combination. The excitement in media circles about the fascinating woman who had descended on the staid fashion environs of New Delhi was continual. The role that the press played in my mother's stardom cannot be underestimated. Both the national and international press pursued her equally. Amongst the innumerable programmes on her, she was featured on the CNN international channel and the BBC made an extremely engaging documentary film on her. Photographer Richard Cameron spent several days with Shahnaz taking candid shots of her life. 'Just go about your work, your life and try and forget all about me,' he'd say. He had this way of turning invisible and just when you thought he wasn't around, the sound of a camera-click would remind you that he was still working hard at his subject.

The red-brick building at the cross-section of two roads became a nerve centre of activity. The spiral staircase leading down from my mother's office into the salon always had an element of impending excitement, because at any time, my mother would appear and be seen dramatically descending the steps, making it a pleasant surprise for the waiting clients.

On this particular day the atmosphere was even more charged than usual, indicating that some very special visitors were expected. A group of clients were taking consultation and some others waited their turn. Suddenly my mother appeared at the top of the staircase and looked down, her eyes surveying every detail that came in the way of her gaze. A moment later, the front door swung open and a lanky blonder-than-blonde beauty with the most infectious smile, walked in. The cameras followed her as she went up to a client and said, 'Hi, I am Goldie Hawn. Are you enjoying your beauty treatment?' Then she saw my mother and her arms flew open. 'Shahnaz,' she said at the top of her voice, 'I have come all the way from the U.S. just to meet you.'

Goldie Hawn wished and hugged everyone in sight and her zest was so incredible that it filled the room with a palpable energy. She embraced twelve-year-old Zubek, who for years later, kept her picture in his room and called her 'my girl'. She had come to record a reality show and interview all rolled in one and the next few hours saw the iconic Hollywood star chatting with my mother, her feet curled up on the sofa, amidst the hum of people going about their work. At the end of the interview, she asked, 'Shahnaz, can I see the other floors too?'

Walking past the living room her ears caught the strains of some Hindi music and she broke into an impromptu dance, her lovely untamed curls bouncing to the beats of Bhangra rock as Sameer showed her the moves of the dance. Soon everyone was inspired enough to join in with this visitor who had brought more than a hint of sunshine with her. When she left, she waved goodbye beaming out from the car window and blew kisses in the air, with the cameras still rolling.

My mother firmly believes that each satisfied customer is worth a million advertisements, especially one who has been liberated from a skin or hair problem that may have changed the way the world looked at her and the way she looked at the world.

Rather than create flashy advertisements that claim overnight miracles, Shahnaz Herbals showed its customers what it could do for them and then let them decide for themselves.

The effects of advertising are often short-term. Companies concentrate too much on instant recognition and glitz instead of focusing on their product, which is the only way to bring in sustainability. Their burst in sales is sometimes limited to the period that the campaign runs. Although quick-fix chemical peels and drastic treatments may seem tempting, natural products have an enduring quality that makes users feel good about themselves. The customers embraced not only the product but also the entire belief system because what Shahnaz Husain was bringing to them was not just a jar of cream but a way of life that was wholesome and inspired by Nature.

While my mother worked with determination to build her career, Sameer laboured on with his aspirations for his music album. After a few intense years of composing and writing his own music, he felt ready to launch his career as a singer on the national scene. He went to Mumbai carrying his music with him and made presentations to some of the biggest music companies there. Magnasound was impressed with his signature style of rap and felt he had a lot of potential. He signed a contract with the company and was extremely excited about his launch. He met with image consultants who told him that his slim frame and long hair made him look more like Yanni than a rap singer. They helped him put together a new look and wardrobe and though it may have been appropriate professionally, we missed Sameer's old poetic persona. I felt the manufactured look took away the real Sameer we were used to.

My mother always remained supportive and respected Sameer's wish to choose music as his profession. She would fly down for his recordings and video shoots to give him moral support; she knew her presence meant a lot to him. When his music was released, Sameer revelled in watching himself on MTV and Channel V. His music was strong and charismatic but I think it was a little ahead of its time. At that point it seemed that he had a long way to go; that there were many albums to create before reaching the top; that this was just the beginning of his career.

The Wind Beneath Her Wings

He was the wind beneath her wings. If she flew high it was because often she caught the gale force of his strength. In many ways his presence was like the arms of a banyan tree: shielding, protective, all-encompassing. He was the shade in her life and mine too. Theirs was a love story that read like the pages of a romantic novel. Yet, the tragedy about all beautiful love stories is that one day they must end. Like a song playing on an old gramophone, beautiful and lilting, the words weaving sweet dreams in which you lose yourself to the music; your limbs submit to its compelling rhythms and just when you become one with the flow of energy and mistake it for eternity, the song ends, leaving only silence. Shaken, you realize the needle of the old gramophone is scratching an empty groove.

My father often remarked that the world must envy us. I think he meant that things never remain blissful for long and as time surges forward, it devours the present. We must hold on to every moment and cherish it, for it never comes back.

My parents had just returned from a long stay in London in 1998 and the house resounded with joy and laughter as shopping bags were opened to reveal gifts for friends and family. There were bags of chocolates for the grandchildren and my favourite angel cake from Marks that my mother always brought back for me. Company executives stood by, eager to catch up with their boss. Amidst all the excitement, I remember noticing my father sitting quietly on the bed. He looked as though he wanted to say something but the words couldn't make it past his lips.

That evening, my mother called me to say that they were having friends over for dinner and asked if Tabrik and I would join them. I agreed immediately, which was something I didn't do too often, since Tabrik was never keen on late nights and I had long ago removed myself from my parents' frequent social evenings. But somehow, that day, I said yes without checking with Tabrik.

Like all my parents' parties this one too had gone from being a quiet dinner with a few friends to a large gathering of business associates, friends and family, all walking in and out of the different rooms. Cosy groups of people sat in the 'pink bedroom', lounging on the bed and chatting, while others filled the 'White House' – the informal living room that opened into a discotheque complete with strobe lights and a professional music system. The house was filled with laughter and conversation. My father showed none of the tiredness of the morning and was in the brightest of spirits, taking to the dance floor every now and then. When he saw me standing by the door, he said, 'Aren't you going to dance with me?' to which I just smiled.

Perhaps I should have taken him up on his offer, since that would have been the last time I would have danced with him.

As the party wound down, I began saying goodbye to the innumerable guests. I had reached the steps when I realized that I had forgotten to wish my father goodbye. Tabrik had already bounded down the spiral staircase, so instead of turning back I told myself that I would see him the next day and apologize.

I woke up at seven the next morning to the insistent ringing of the telephone. When I answered, the voice at the other end said, 'Sahib is not well. Please come quickly.'

My grip on the receiver tightened as I asked, 'Has he had a heart attack?'

It was my worst nightmare; I expected to hear, '*No, Madam. He is just feverish*' or something.

The voice on the phone shattered my hopes, 'Yes, Madam.'

Trembling in disbelief, I repeated my question but the answer did not change. As nightmarish as it felt, it was stark reality. I pulled on a robe and holding Tabrik's hand I got into the car. My mind was racing as I got hold of the phone number of the eminent cardiologist Dr Naresh Trehan and called him from the car.

He knew my parents only as acquaintances so I was not quite sure whether he would respond but he did and I will always remain grateful to him for that. He said he would meet us at the nearby nursing home where my father had already been taken.

When Tabrik and I reached the nursing home, my mother rushed to me with Sameer by her side to assure me that my father was recovering and that the doctors were with him. By a strange twist of fate, the very house we had lived in as a young family, where we had shared so many happy moments together – W-33 – had been converted into a nursing home where my father was now struggling for his life. The nice landlady's son had become a cardiologist and he was battling to save my father.

It was unnerving. My eyes scanned the walls of my childhood home and I asked myself if this was what was destined – that my father should return to the home of his youth for his final moments. I gazed through a veil of tears at the silent hillock and temple that I had woken up to each morning as a six-year-old. When Dr Trehan arrived we rushed to him with that sense that one feels when hope is thin and the doctor appears like an agent of God. My father was moved to the Escorts Heart Institute where he was operated upon for 99 per cent blockage in his arteries.

Many hours later, as we waited outside the ICU, Zubek asked if 'Delhi Papa' was awake. That was the first time we wondered why he had not come out of anaesthesia after all this time. Apparently, though the surgery had been a success, the damage that had occurred in the first few minutes was irreversible. My father's brain had been deprived of oxygen for too long, causing brain death. Although denial seemed comforting we were forced to accept the possibility that he would never wake up from the blissful sleep in which he lay.

For the first time in her life, my mother looked completely shattered. She had met my father when she was fourteen and had been married to him for forty-one years. He had been her anchor for almost her entire life and in one unsuspecting moment she had become rudderless. Dr Trehan had a consulting room near the ICU opened up for us and we sat there in silent vigil as sorrow seeped into our hearts.

On the fourth night, I remember lying on the bed in the consulting room while my mother lay quietly on the couch. In the steely darkness, I saw my father, luminescent in the eye of my mind, walking by the side of the lake as I went boating in Nainital. 'Is that your father following our boat on foot?' my perplexed friend had asked. 'Yes, that is my father,' I had said and smiled. That was indeed my protective father. Every time I went horse riding I would see him turning up to watch me safely dismount. 'Don't worry, Papa,' I would say. 'I won't fall.'

How I wished that I could do something to protect him today. If only I could.

At that moment the door opened and an apologetic intern brought the inevitable news. We rushed to my father's side just as the luminous light in the monitor flatlined into a long horizontal one, which in my mind is the beginning of the journey to another world, where saints and the nicest people live.

It was on the seventh of September 1998 that my father passed away, as gently as he had lived, leaving a terrible void. That night changed me forever. I ensured that my traumatized mother and brother got some sleep, I asked Tabrik to take care of young Zubek, who was shaken by his grandfather's death and I personally made all the arrangements for the funeral of my dad with an armour of steel over my heart.

There were articles about him in the papers the next day that spoke of his grace and kindness, his generosity and elegance; the one I treasure most and hope to show to my grandchildren one day was a feature in the *Mid-day* entitled 'Passing of a Gentleman'.

I had never seen my mother look so frail and vulnerable. Clad in all black, with a veil around her face, it pained me to see her in grief. I slept with her for several nights after Papa's death and we would chat till the wee hours of the morning, pouring our feelings into the void.

'Mum, you are so young. Do you think you will marry again someday?' I said to her a few weeks later.

'Don't say that,' she said, almost offended.

'I am serious, Mum; I will find someone for you. I promise I will.' The roles were changing; I was turning protective, almost motherly, in my concern for her. I wanted to mend my mother's life.

In the months that followed, her loneliness and grief became increasingly marked. She looked as though she was at sea,

completely lost and without direction. Her friends were supportive
and rallied by her side. Her long-time confidante Vyjayanthimala
Bali flew down from Chennai to be with her, but no one could
substitute a life partner of forty years.

Weighed down by her grief, my mother stopped going to office.
For the first time in her life, even her work did not interest her.
When someone has been an extension of yourself for so long,
losing him is like losing a part of your body. 'If you lose a hand
or a leg, you carry on somehow but you will always miss that part
of yourself,' she admitted to Vir Sanghvi in an interview for the
BBC. It was a very touching moment. As I watched the show,
I saw a film of tears glistening in my mother's eyes, which she
managed to hold back and move quickly on to another topic.

One of the visitors she met during this time was Deepak
Chopra, the spiritual guru to Hollywood. He spoke to my mother
at length about his centre where he conducted many therapeutic
courses and my mother seemed inclined to visit the U.S. for a
spiritual experience for a while but then she realized that it was
here and within that all the answers existed.

Although I was the President of the company and had worked
with my mother almost every day of my life – met buyers in
her absence, handled production and marketing and worked in
the R&D department – I had always shied away from making a
complete commitment to the business. I had revelled in my days
of freedom, enjoying my time with my sons and Tabrik, travelling
the world and doing as I pleased. Casually dressed in stretch pants,
T-shirts and flip-flops, I looked as different from my mother as
could be imagined. Looking at me, my brother had once remarked,
'Every time I look at Appi, I feel it's a Sunday.'

Yes! Indeed if a nickname had to be chosen for me in that particular phase of my life it would have been 'Sunday'. The day my father passed away all that changed. I simply got up the next morning and walked into the office. There was no formal induction, no discussions; it is just in the natural order of things that when you are the eldest and you are called on to pick up the mantle, you do so instinctively. I moved my father's table and brown leather chair to my room and felt his energy and his blessings radiate through them.

I noticed some of the company executives walking around in casual T-shirts in the office, something that had never happened in my father's lifetime. I immediately called one of them in and said that there had been a dress code in the company for many years and it was not about to change. It was the first time I asserted myself and it was a sign to all in our company that we were down but not out. The control was back in place and I was holding the reins of the business that my mother had built, protecting it as though it were my life.

Leaving the company in my hands, my mother left for London with some close friends for company. She needed to get away from the city where she couldn't walk down the road without being stopped by people offering their condolences. In her absence, I finally began managing the business by myself for the first time. I took over the national distribution network and have handled it ever since. Perhaps, I did not learn sword-fencing at Rahat Manzil, yet I managed life's challenges with the courage of women before me.

While in London, my mother took sessions with a trauma specialist but nothing seemed to bring her peace or acceptance of her loss. We were all getting extremely concerned about her.

We heard that she had stopped eating and walked aimlessly for miles, with her loyal maid following her. When she returned after her extended stay in London she was sixteen kilos slimmer, emotionally exhausted but looking more fragile and beautiful than ever.

On her return, we began the difficult task of trying to cheer her up. We would drag her to weddings and insist she join us on the dance floor. My brother, who was an encyclopaedia of jokes and had the ability to leave a room full of sober people in splits, would come up with his best ones and we all laughed harder than we ever had. But the echoes remained hollow. It seemed nothing less than a miracle would raise my mother's spirits.

Without my father by her side, life had changed so drastically that sometimes I despaired, thinking she would never find the inspiration to smile again. I realized that perhaps the comfort and confidence she had developed in my ability to handle the company was encouraging her to stay away from the only thing that could be her saviour at this point, her work. Her passion for Shahnaz Herbals needed to be reawakend.

'Mummy, I need to go to Mumbai for a while to be with my in-laws,' I said one day. She looked a little surprised and I felt a pang of guilt, but it was the correct decision. When I returned in two weeks' time, she was in office handling the company with some of the old zest back in her.

Shahnaz Herbals could never replace my father, yet it had the capacity to bring hope, it was almost like the presence of a growing child in our lives.

When the Future Came She Was Already There

There was complete silence in the pure white room; with the lights shining on her face, she looked into the lens with the nonchalance of a pro. 'Shahnaz, how is your company going to face up to the innumerable multinational brands that are coming to India?'

My mother smiled at the young lady who had asked the question. 'I don't have to face them. They are coming to my country, they will have to face *me*.'

Over the years, the company had seen changes in trade policies and market upheavals but none as significant as the coming of economic liberalization. By now the impact was being felt strongly. India had opened its doors to the world and as international companies came in, a steady stream of glamorous models walked off television screens and into the somewhat tentative Indian psyche. No one was quite sure what would work in this unexposed and untried market. While brands jostled with each other for space in the Indian market, Shahnaz Herbals carefully distanced itself from the chaos.

Personally, I was in favour of riding the wave. I tried several times to convince my mother to consider the offers of tie-ups that were pouring in from multinational companies and felt that it was essential to flow with the changing business environment but she was unbending in her resolve. Her vision for the future had clarity and confidence. She felt that it was time to consolidate the brand rather than dilute its image by collaborating with a company that her customers were not familiar with. Perhaps my father's absence made her feel particularly uncomfortable at the thought of creating new associations.

At a time when most domestic enterprises were concerned about their future and some succumbed to the influence of foreign investors, my mother was certain that Shahnaz Herbals would not be affected because we were a brand that dealt with treating skin and hair problems. Over the years she had created a niche for her products and clients who believed in them and in the Shahnaz Husain Promise.

In 1997, my mother appointed me the President of the company. I accepted the position like a blessing and have treated it as my life's most sacred gift. The presidency of the company brought with it responsibilities and commitment but when you are born to a chosen one, you cannot walk away from your destiny.

I took my mother's decision to consolidate the company as a challenge. The path of going it alone required invention and creativity. To keep pace with a dynamic market it was essential to develop new and revolutionary products. My personal forté and passion has always been product development; I thrive on the process of research and development, long discussions with chemists, smelling and feeling ingredients and choosing the most effective ones with which to create bestselling products. The distillation equipment fascinates me most of all. When you put in a fresh herb, root, leaf or flower and watch it being processed through the glass unit, until it is finally delivered as pure essence, you feel a sense of its purity and goodness. Shahnaz Herbals factories stock at least 150 different herbs and oils at any time. I feel it's time we displayed them with our products, as I have done at the Shahnaz Husain Signature Store at the Select Citywalk Mall in Saket, Delhi. Customers are fascinated to actually see the herbs that go into a product they are applying on themselves.

On one of my trips to London I was scouting for ideas and visited innumerable book shops to find new, untapped material on Ayurveda. Finally, it was in the basement of the London bookshop Foyle's that I picked up an old copy of a classic on Ayurveda; bound in deep green, slightly damp and musty from being left untouched. It was like finding a gem, one that was waiting to be read by me. Going through its contents, I found a chapter on 'swarana' – gold. As I read about the powerful, age-controlling properties of the timeless metal and its impact on skin rejuvenation, I sat up in excitement. I called up my mother and told her of my amazing discovery.

I returned to India and along with a team of Ayurvedic chemists plunged into the compelling journey of product development. The final result was hugely satisfying; the thought of a skin product made from pure gold created an instant stir in the market.

Being a treatment line, packaging had always been low priority at Shahnaz Herbals but the container of the 24-Carat Gold Skin Radiance Gel was unique in its design. Shaped like a transparent disc, it sat in the palm of one's hand and radiated a sense of its inherent precious quality. It also carried a purity certification stamp that gave consumers added confidence of quality. Within weeks of its launch, the 24-Carat Gold range had increased the company's sales by 20 per cent. It was my first milestone in my mother's company and I was thrilled at its phenomenal success. Today we are aware that the company's ability to innovate has put it on the watch-list of international companies. La Prairie the well-known Swiss skin-care brand sells a pure gold radiance serum at $580, which is about thirty thousand rupees for a 30 ml. bottle. I feel it is commendable that R&D at Shahnaz Herbals is of international standards and its impact on global trends is possibly more far-reaching than most people would imagine.

Often a product is developed to cater to a need. The feedback from our centres showed that there was a persistent demand for a highly specialized fairness cream made from natural sources. I worked on developing a fairness cream with the idea of offering a natural option to women who were using chemical products. The Pearl Skin-Whitening cream was launched as a top-of-the-line fairness product and once again the response from users was enthusiastic. It was surprising that though ample literature existed to show that pearl powder slowed down the production of melanin and while it had been used in China for years, no major domestic or international company had explored its potential.

Though Ayurveda is primarily associated with plants, some of its most powerful formulations are found in rocks and minerals. Shahnaz Herbals is the only company that explored the mineral formulations in Ayurveda. The Diamond range was developed after seeing the amazing results and customer acceptance of the Gold range. Once again, this is an ancient formulation in which 'bhasma', the potent mineral ash that is produced when diamonds are fired, is used. The newest launch amongst the Premium products has been the Platinum range. Developed with nano technology to minimize the size of the particles and make them fine enough to penetrate the skin, it is a strong age-control formulation.

Amongst the important releases for the mass market this year is Shahnaz Herbals' acne-control gel. Created especially for youngsters, it has been named 'Oops'. Strong chemical formulations used on young skins may remove pimples quickly but they normally leave behind a nagging dark spot. Oops is an excellent product made from natural ingredients that are kind to the skin and tough on acne. It removes pimples and leaves the skin blemish-free.

The influence my mother has had on the Ayurvedic and cosmetic industry in India has been phenomenal; the inspirational effect that she has had on it, the path she has shown, has many keen followers. The company's ability to invent, innovate and bring in new products has made it a trailblazer for imitators. When once asked about the many clones she has spawned, my mother replied, 'The best compliment for any original is the copies.'

Research and development at Shahnaz Herbals continues even as I write. It is a process that must never and can never, stop. Imagination, the wealth of past knowledge, latest testing techniques and experience come together to create purely natural products that are not only effective but also unmatched by any others in the market.

Autumn Love

The sorrow in my mother's eyes still remained. Though she had settled down to an uneasy routine, smiled perfunctorily and made attempts at rejuvenating her enthusiasm, the pain of her loss lingered. It came up in small things; when his favourite dish was cooked in the house; when she had a problem at work that she would normally turn to him to handle; when she heard his favourite ghazal, '*Zindagi mein toh sabhi pyaar kiya kartein hain/ Mein toh mar kar bhi meri jaan tujjhe chahoonga...*' His presence, his memory, was always with her like a shadow. Yet the matrix of ironies was working in unexpected ways to restore her happiness.

With my father no longer around to guide it, the company needed an efficient and capable structure. We approached A.F. Ferguson and Co., a renowned consultancy firm. Mr Puri, a senior partner, visited us to discuss ways in which my mother could professionalize Shahnaz Herbals. Until then my father had taken care of a major chunk of the workload and with the two of them together at the helm my parents had successfully managed the affairs of the company. But in recent months it had become obvious that without a stronger professional hierarchy it would be hard to function.

As they talked about the structure of the company and discussed the best way to consolidate it, my mother spoke to Mr Puri about my father and how much he had supported her in her work. Touched by her circumstances, Mr Puri revealed that he as well had experienced a similar loss recently; his wife of many years had succumbed to cancer after a four-year-long struggle, around the same time that my father had passed away. He offered to lend my mother the book he was reading, *Life after Death*, which had helped him cope with his bereavement.

Destiny was gently steering them towards each other; the stars propelling them on their preordained path. Over the next few months, Mr Puri and my mother met often and as they talked about their shared sense of loss, they found that they understood each other's grief as no one else could. Their professional relationship slowly transformed into a friendship based on mutual admiration and respect. My mother would often confide her feelings in me through those days and I became her best friend and her confidante more than ever.

One day she walked into my office looking preoccupied. While we sat sipping warm tea from oversized mugs she lowered her voice and told me that Mr Puri had proposed to her. I was really happy to hear this. From what I knew of him, I felt Mr Puri would finally bring my mother happiness and strength; that he would be the perfect anchor for her rudderless life. I felt a sense of peace knowing that my lovely mother would not be alone any more.

It so happened, that the date the registrar gave for the wedding coincided with my son's stay in hospital post a gall bladder surgery he required. My mother was torn but I insisted that she not change the date or tamper with the course of events in any way. With our son in the Apollo Hospital, I did not think that I could expect Tabrik to understand my compulsions, so I decided it would be best to keep the news from him.

On the day that my mother married Mr Raj Puri, I left the hospital, went home, changed into a formal sari and on my way to M-86 I stopped by at the Swarovski showroom and picked up their famous crystal star as a wedding present for my mother and Mr Puri. It was a sombre moment but nevertheless a joyous one. My mother looked pretty and elegant in beige and gold, while Mr Puri was clad in his hallmark pin-striped suit. Surrounded by their children and a few close family members, they signed the register and solemnized their relationship into the sacred bond of marriage.

I saw my mother smile again and my eyes turned moist with a multitude of emotions. I felt my mother's marriage to Mr Puri was an act of providence. How else could one explain two people, alone and in grief, finding one another at a time when they needed each other most? It was clear that it was a survival instinct, a desire to reclaim their happiness and live in the protective embrace of each other's shade, that brought them together.

When I sat in the car to rush back to the hospital I slouched in the seat, exhausted with the pace of changing events. I missed my anchor.

'What kept you so long?' asked Tabrik as I walked into the hospital room wearing a simple cotton kurta.

'Oh, just some unavoidable issues at Mum's,' I replied without looking him in the eye. The open and honest relationship we share with each other made it difficult for me to lie to him but sitting next to our son who was recovering from his surgery I could not bring myself to tell him of the wedding. I was also aware that he only needed to meet Mr Puri once to realize why I had the confidence to want to see him by my mother's side forever. I was right. A few weeks later, when I introduced the two men, they got along extremely well and remain good friends.

My mother's marriage to Mr Puri was a perfect decision. It was wonderful to see her effervescence and zest for life return. The void that had come into her life had now been filled.

Mr Puri is very different from the way my father was and yet I see so many similarities. They both belong to a time and culture that produced articulate, compassionate and generous men. My father was a gentleman from Lucknow with finesse and charm, while Mr Puri is an impeccably dressed westernized gentleman. He was born in the U.K. where he lived for many years. After completing his chartered accountancy in England he returned to India and joined Ferguson where he went on to become a senior partner of the firm.

Mr Puri is always polite, opens the door for my mother and has the genteel mannerisms of a British aristocrat. He is also extremely considerate and very liberal in his ideas, which I think are rare qualities. He has brought a lot of happiness to my mother and indeed to the whole family.

In 2003 my mother decided to finally reward herself with a private home; a place where she could cut herself away from her work. Over the years she had allowed her personal space to be intruded on by her profession but now things needed to change. Mr Puri is a very private person and my mother respected his nature. On a corner plot in W Block, Greater Kailash, not far from her first home years ago, she built an elegant house where she now lives. She has named it Bramblebush Cottage.

Incredibly, Bramblebush Cottage was cloned from a pottery piece that my mother had picked up at the Sunday flea market at Covent Garden in London. She held it up in her hand and said: 'This is what I want my home to look like,' beaming like a child at her astonished architect. She has retained her ability to chase dreams as though they were butterflies until they were in her grasp. Bramblebush cottage, which once sat on the shelf of a cart in a weekend market in London, is one such dream that she chased and sculpted into reality.

This fresh beginning and home was indeed my mother's destiny. Incredibly, many years ago my mother was in Pune to inaugurate a Shahnaz Herbal salon. The *Times of India* carried an advertisement to say that she was visiting the city and would be giving consultations. A lady who was in Pune for a short trip from Mumbai opened the morning papers and was thrilled to read the ad. She had always been a fan of the beauty diva and the possibility of meeting her in person was very tempting. She requested her husband to drive her down so that she could have a private consultation with the expert. The indulgent husband agreed and the couple got into their car and drove to the centre. There were rows of men waiting in the reception and the husband joined them and sat patiently while his wife met Shahnaz Husain.

She described her problems and Shahnaz gave her expert opinion. 'What did you say your name was?' she asked the lady as she wrote out a prescription.

'Kamlesh,' said the lovely lady. 'Kamlesh Puri.'

The two women looked at each other and smiled pleasantly, unaware of the strange intricacies that the future held for them.

Harvard Days

When she had walked out of St. Mary's school in Allahabad at the age of sixteen to marry her first love, little could Shahnaz have imagined that her next academic foray would be a course in business negotiations at Harvard, many decades later. The absence of a formal education had remained an unfulfilled ambition through the years that she rose to become India's leading businesswoman.

While professors from Harvard had visited her often to gain an insight into her business techniques and she had spoken to students at the London School of Economics, she still felt wistful about missing out on a formal college education. It had been one of her deepest regrets.

Today, a lifetime later, she was keeping her promise to her father. After attending President Obama's summit of outstanding world entrepreneurs, my mother and Mr Puri took a flight from Washington D.C. to Boston on an invitation to speak at Harvard, where she had also enrolled herself as a student. Driving through the gates of the university, she was ready to complete the one unfulfilled ambition that had remained. Her heart was beating hard. For the first time in years she felt a little nervous. She had forgotten what it was like to sit in a class, to obey commands and conform to rules.

Mr Puri looked at her with a reassuring smile. 'Don't worry. You will be fine.'

On her first day at Harvard she got off the car and headed straight for the office where she filled in her form. With her eye on the watch she made a quick dash to the lecture hall but to her complete dismay she was five minutes too late and the doors had been shut. It seemed that she would have to wait a lifetime and a day to sit in a college room.

She returned to the admissions office where the helpful advisor explained, 'I am so sorry, Ms Husain but you have missed the morning session and though you can sit for the rest of the course we will not be able to give you a certificate at the end of your time with us.'

My mother looked disappointed and it showed in her eyes. 'I was late by just five minutes.'

'Indeed, but we are bound by our rules.'

'This is very important to me,' said my mother and then lowering her voice she added, 'I must get a certificate. Can you suggest another course for me, please?' The lady clicked the keys of her computer and peered through her glasses. 'I do have something very interesting for you but you will have to fly to Harvard at Hertfordshire in England for that. This is a course for CEO's and entrepreneurs and it starts in two weeks.'

'Then book me for that one as well, please. I will complete the course at Boston and then fly down to be in time for the session at Hertfordshire.'

As she was returning dejectedly to the hotel she chanced upon the students' store and walked in to browse through the many college souvenirs it stocked. 'Can I help you, Madam?' asked a salesgirl.

211

'Yes,' she said. 'Give me one of everything.'

The salesgirl looked shocked. 'Madam, we stock a lot of items. Are you quite sure you want *every* one of them?' she asked.

My mother is a chronic shopaholic and even at Harvard shopping remained an instinct with her.

The next morning she was up at six, anxious not to be late. She packed her Harvard satchel bag, placed a set of notebooks, pencils and sharpeners all neatly in place and then, along with Tayab – her Jeeves from India – she headed back to college. The early morning streets of Boston were filled with students and she felt good to be walking amongst them. This time the doors were wide open; in fact she was the first to arrive. She sat in the multilevel lecture hall that accommodated a hundred students at a time and smiled. It was a smile that started in her heart and travelled through her soul to appear on her lips. She felt a rush of adrenaline as the students began to pour in, some casually waving to her. 'Hi,' said a boy with curly dark hair. 'I am Jerry and I am from Morocco.'

My mother was a little nonplussed. 'Shahnaz, from India,' she replied.

When the professor walked in, the class immediately grew silent and completely attentive. After introducing himself, he started the course on business negotiations: 'The most important part of any business is the power to negotiate correctly. Good negotiators are always winners.' My mother took notes as he spoke on. 'Remember,' he said. 'If there is a chance of getting a negative response in any situation, don't ask. Just go ahead and do it and take your chance.'

That seemed like good advice.

The next morning my mother was there half an hour early and with Tayab's able assistance she put a small sample of Shahnaz

Herbals' Diamond cream along with a company brochure on each table. The class was curious and quite excited with the gift. The professor walked in and observed the excitement.

'Ms Husain, promotional material is not allowed in the class.'

'Sir,' said my mother, 'I was only putting into practice what you taught us yesterday. When in doubt of a negative response you had said just go ahead and do it.'

The class broke into peals of laughter and the professor smiled. 'Quick learner, Ms Husain. Quick learner for sure.'

It was not long before my mother became the most popular student in her class and would often be seen sitting at lunch with a group of students around her, enthralling them with anecdotes of her life and giving them advice on treating their skin and hair problems with natural sources. She created a sense of fascination and curiosity. There were questions on the colour of her hair, the gold anklets she wore, on her early marriage. *'What?* You got engaged at fourteen? Married at sixteen? That's unbelievable. Was it a forced marriage?'

'No, it wasn't,' said Mum, a smile on her lips. 'I loved him.'

It is believed that those with a higher EQ or emotional quotient are more successful at business. In Harvard that is how they would probably describe her success.

The farewell at Boston was a moonlight dinner where my mother exchanged addresses with her group of students and said her goodbyes to friends she had made in the corridors of Harvard. At the end of the course, she gave her scheduled lecture and spoke on 'Achieving Success without Advertising'. She went through two experiences in this enriching trip – she was both a student as well as an honoured speaker. As the group of 400 students listened attentively she ended her speech with the touching insight she often shares with the young and the ambitious: 'If I am asked for my advice on achieving success, I would say this: follow your heart.'

The applause was strong and brimming with approval. Clearly, here was a lady who had an almost spiritual sense for business.

The end of one Harvard course was the beginning of another. Determined to acquire a degree, she flew across the Atlantic, driving directly from the airport to Harvard at Hertfordshire where she and Mr Puri checked into a hotel that had been taken over by the university for its students.

This time my mother made sure that she was half an hour early for every class. The profile at the CEO's course was very different. Here, there were heads of leading companies, each with their own engaging experiences and the lunchtime interactions were as educational as the classes. There was also a session in which each participant recalled their business story and it was interesting to hear the inventive ideas and methods that were used to achieve success in different countries and cultures.

The final day of the course at Harvard was momentous for my mother. She sat with Mr Puri by her side in the ornate auditorium for the convocation ceremony. This was the day she had waited for, for a lifetime.

'Shahnaz Husain,' announced the voice on the mike. My mother walked up on stage to hold in her hands a certificate from Harvard. As she returned to her seat her eyes brimmed with tears. She remembered her father more than ever and the single thought that played through her mind was, 'Papa, I wish you could see this.'

When she returned home to Delhi, the Amaltas trees that appeared in the searing heat of early June were a flaming yellow fire. My mother looked out of her bedroom window and smiled. She loved the Amaltas tree outside her window and today it was in its perfect moment of bloom, its laden branches within touching distance from the first-floor balcony at Bramblebush Cottage. Life had moved through several stages and with it each home had become a distinct landmark on the winding path of her journey.

That day, the blooming of the Amaltas at Bramblebush Cottage was reason enough to delay her appointments, just so she could sit with Mr Puri on the balcony and take in the splendid sight. She asked her staff to lay out the tea on the table and went in to dress. The intercom rang. Mr Kutty was on the line to inform her that the Korean delegation was coming in and that their appointment could not be cancelled.

The Amaltas waited every morning. My mother promised to keep a date with it but each day her life took over. One day she looked out of the window at the stark yellow blaze and asked her staff why they hadn't put the tea out on the balcony. 'That was last year, Madam,' came the reply.

My mother was silent for a moment, shocked at the pace of her life. A year had passed, the Amaltas was blooming once again and life was racing ahead of the seasons. It is an incident she feels represents the hectic momentum of her life. Perhaps it is time to stop and wait and just look at the flowers and keep her date with the Amaltas tree.

The Young Turk Enters

The handsome young man sitting in front of me was trying to catch my attention as I flipped through the mail that arrived on my table each morning. The fragrance of freshly brewed coffee lingered in the air as he sipped his sugarless brew. 'That's what America did to you,' I said. 'Got you hooked onto black coffee for life.'

'Oh, Mum, look at your mug, it's like liquid pudding,' retorted Sharik.

He had just returned after five long years, having completed his education at Columbia University in New York, where he had studied Economics and then spent some time working in the Big Apple. His time away from home had brought about a quantum change in him – there was an air of confidence about him, a mental growth and vision. But I was happy and relieved to see that he had retained the values of the land where he was born.

Sending your nineteen-year-old to an environment completely unlike your own, to navigate his way through the different circumstances he would find himself in with no family guidance to fall back on, hoping that the traditions you brought him up with will remain largely unaffected and he will bring back in him the best of what he experiences is a risk but for Sharik it had worked out well.

'So, Mum, what do you think I should do about my career?' he asked, trying to draw my attention to the fact that he was about to become an earning member of the family.

'Join the company,' I said casually, knowing quite well that the worst thing I could do was to pressurize him into something he was not ready for.

'I want to stick to my speciality; I want to remain in finance,' he said. 'I think I want to expand New Ratings.'

New Ratings was a financial website that he and a group of students had started at Columbia; even though it was in its nascent stage it had already been listed in the San Francisco papers as one of the top ten websites to look out for.

'Go ahead, follow your dreams,' I said, secretly hoping that he would return to work at Shahnaz Herbals one day. I wished I could tell him that he was the future of the company that his grandmother had devoted her life to building but I had to let him explore, fly unhindered till he found his way back home, where he belonged.

For the next year, Sharik focused on New Ratings. The website succeeded beyond his wildest dreams and soon there were several offers from leading companies to buy the website. I was not quite sure whether he should sell it or hold on to it like his first gold medal but his partners and he decided to sell out. Having experienced the pleasure that comes with personal achievement he now looked more comfortable with the road ahead.

Once more, we sat opposite each other, with the fragrance of coffee lingering in the air. 'What do you think I should do now?' he asked.

'Join the company,' I suggested and held my breath.

He looked into his coffee mug for a long minute, contemplating. 'Well, maybe I will,' he said finally, with a smile that deepened his dimples.

I heaved a sigh of relief and walked across to my mother's room where she sat surrounded by animal skin upholstery, glistening crystal and the trappings of success, with the most priceless news.

'Mum! Sharik has agreed to join the business,' I said, my voice unable to contain my excitement.

A smile flashed across my mother's face as she realized that the chain that links any personal achievement to the unseen future had been established.

When time overlaps time there is a confluence of ideas, a boundless flow of creativity. When three generations work together in a business the result is a fine blend of thoughts, ambitions, advice and experience. When youth gets over-adventurous, experience holds back and when experience becomes overconfident, someone who has been the bridge between the two strives towards a balanced perspective. I also believe that we have as much to learn from the next generation, as we have to give them of our experiences. I also believe in accommodating their dreams within the larger picture, ensuring that they find personal satisfaction and completeness in what they do; creating the space to allow their own fantasies and watching with happiness as they find themselves within the company. A company that is flexible enough to blend in every child's dream and make it its own, is a winner through time.

My mother was the pioneer of Shahnaz Herbals. It was her vision, her plan, that shaped itself into the reality that it is today but over the years her support systems have changed. Each one of us has made a distinct contribution to the growth of the company with our own dreams and our own style. When my mother first started Shahnaz Herbals my father was the driving force by her side. Everything, from the packaging to the products, bore his mark in some way or the other, till one day he was no more. That was when I joined the business wholeheartedly and brought my own thoughts and influences to the company, focusing my energies on research and development.

My mother and I worked together for many years and I think we managed the business fairly well. While she was fiery and ambitious, I was methodical and calm. She loved people and the press, for me they were an intrusion in a good day's work. While she found immense fame, I think I collected a lot of goodwill. Together we were a good balance.

Sharik's entry into the company in 2005 brought my mother the kind of joy and enthusiasm I had not seen in her in a long time. They travelled together on business trips and sat for hours discussing company policy and strategies. She saw in his unconditional dedication to his work what she had missed in me, torn as I always was between my family and my responsibility to the company.

The presence of a young man who had the future clearly etched out in his mind brought with it a new professionalism that began to speak for itself. The business graph was moving up, new sales points were added and my mother's concept of personal consultation was being renewed by beauty advisors at all major outlets. His ability to open out new markets and forge relationships in countries like Korea, Myanmar and South Africa made him the company's deal-maker at a very early stage. The factories that had expanded from Okhla to Noida and Dehradun were all working to full capacity and it was decided that we would now build a brand new state-of-the-art facility in the foothills of the Shivalik ranges.

The factory in Roorkee has been Sharik's pet project and is equipped with the latest technologies and the most modern machinery. Automation has lessened work hours, increased capacity and created efficiency. 'I am looking ten years ahead,' he said when asked why Shahnaz Herbals needed such advanced equipment.

Today Shahnaz Herbals employs 1800 people at various levels, exports to sixty countries, has a repertoire of 250 products produced in factories spread over three states, 400 franchise salons and 50,000 points of sale, making it a front-runner in the natural care and cure segment. The brand's formidable position is an endorsement of the faith that clients have in the quality and efficacy of the products.

Zubek has been initiated into the business as well and has brought to it his own expertise in technology. He has recently launched 'Shastore' a retail website for Shahnaz Herbals' products, which intends to root out the mostly spurious versions sold on the net. Internet sales are going to be a vital part of any company's growth in the future and he will ensure that Shahnaz Herbals remains tech-savvy and in sync with the purchasing habits of the new generation. Zubek has a highly refined intellect and conversations with him are always enriching. He was the political editor of his school magazine and managed to obtain an audience with His Holiness the Dalai Lama, whom he interviewed. He was granted ten minutes but an hour later His Holiness and Zubek were still talking about His Holiness's childhood, his escape from Tibet and his hopes for his people, as the officers stood by waiting impatiently. Philanthropy is Zubek's other passion and I hope he makes Shahnaz Herbals even more socially responsible as a company.

In 2011 a wonderful young lady became a part of all our lives when Sharik found someone he wanted to spend his life with.

Amrita has brought us immense happiness and made us proud grandparents. I am sure the future will bring new ideas and inputs from her as well.

Mr Puri is an able advisor to my mother; his judgement backed by his years at Ferguson. With his ability to handle finance and his wisdom with numbers my mother often seeks his guidance. He is extremely straightforward and uncomplicated in his approach to any issue and I think that is his strongest quality.

Though Tabrik has studiously maintained a distance from the company, my mother's affection for him is obvious. She admires his equanimity and opinion and values the solid and undemonstrative strength that he brings to the family. He has a wonderful equation with her.

Behind every star on stage there are strategic backstage artistes. We have all played a part and continue to do so in this story that is still playing on.

Through the years many things had changed, time had brought new relationships and fresh beginnings into my mother's life. Somehow it was now time to revisit the past once more. The launch of Fair One, Shahnaz Herbals' first mass-marketed product, in Hyderabad in May 2005 became an opportunity to reconnect with our roots. Zubek, who had grown up listening to stories of Hyderabad, was looking forward to the visit, as was Tabrik, though more perhaps for an opportunity to sample the fabled Hyderabadi cuisine.

The trip also gave my mother a chance to introduce Mr Puri to her family, who was his usual charming self and it was nice to see them take to him with warmth.

We stayed at the Sheraton Hotel, where the walls bore huge sepia pictures of the Nizam's days. Munno Aunty, the eldest member of the family, pointed out our ancestors on the walls: *'That's great-grandfather on army sports day and that beautiful lady beside him was your...'* There was an amazing picture of the Nizam's feast that held us all spellbound. It was surreal – dining in a restaurant with our ancestors captured in celluloid stills waltzing all around us, sharing our joy that evening. The two feasts seemed to connect across time and space as we laughed and chatted while great-grandfather smiled his approval.

The next night we dined at Munno Aunty's house, where my mother was the toast of the evening; she had done her family proud and her homecoming was a time for celebration. After a sumptuous dinner of Hyderabadi biryani and other old recipes and family favourites, Uncle Khusro pulled out a scroll of butter paper, a very special surprise for Zubek. It was a huge print of the family tree made by a cousin in California that traced nine hundred members of the Sir Afsar family. To Zubek's surprise he found that his name had been diligently added to the document.

The press in Hyderabad was enthusiastically laying claim to my mother as their 'girl' and the release of the first mass-marketed product in Hyderabad was truly momentous. Though the Pearl Naturally Whitening range had emerged as a strong product line, it addressed the high-end market. Fair One was an important launch for Shahnaz Herbals because it was aimed at the masses and also because the fairness market did not have a strong 'natural' player. My mother had been working on an alternative to the chemical concoctions being used throughout the country. It was not an endorsement of the 'fair is beautiful' misconception in Indian society, which is a deep-rooted social issue and will take time and modernity to address. Fair One was, quite simply, about presenting the consumer with a choice, a natural substitute.

Each new generation of women *and* men inherit a new set of problems and it is important to be sensitive to the needs of the consumer. Work pressure, long hours spent on the road, exposure to carbon emissions, pollutants, late nights, excessive consumption of alcohol, crash dieting and emotional stress are some of the problems that young urban India is struggling with. The desire to keep up with the ever-changing concept of beauty wreaks havoc on people's bodies and minds. Over the years the number of young people coming to our salons with dehydration and fine lines that should have appeared years later has increased and we find ourselves creating and dispensing rich moisturizers and night creams to men and women who have begun to age prematurely, as well as giving advice on the right diet and nutrition.

Beauty is not just about looking good but also about respecting yourself, about finding the perfect balance for your body without compromising your health. At the end of the day, the pursuit of beauty must lead to health and happiness.

Sleep Sweet Prince

Sunday, the twenty-sixth of January 2008, was a perfect sun-kissed winter morning in Delhi, yet I woke up with a strange feeling in the pit of my stomach. Frankly, I felt like birds do before a storm. As the day unfolded itself I realized that perhaps it was an intuition of things to come.

Sameer had been away for a winter break with his family and we were expecting him back the next day. Instead, the phone rang with an incoherent receptionist trying to put disjointed words together.

'What are you trying to say?' I asked in disbelief.

'Sameer Bhaiya has had an accident,' the receptionist repeated, steadying his tone.

My stomach churned and my knees went weak. I virtually slid down the stairs and sank into the white leather sofa where I had sat with my brother just a month ago laughing at his incessant jokes. I felt as though I was trapped in a nightmare. I called up a cousin who lives in Patna and it was clear from his tone that Sameer was in a critical state.

'Where are you, Nelofar?' my mother's voice came from upstairs and I felt my heart sink. My head was spinning and by now some of the staff and my mother's secretary were by my side. I searched for a way to avoid telling my mother what had happened immediately so, steadying my voice and my heart, I spoke to her on the intercom and told her that I was talking to Tabrik and would be up soon. I then called for an ambulance and a doctor so we could deal with the shock she would suffer when she heard the news.

Moments later, Tabrik and Sharik rushed down the driveway. As soon as the doctor arrived, we went up the staircase that led to my mother's private area of the house. She looked around at all the faces, confused, and then I whispered very softly, as if lowering my voice could reduce the impact of the news, that Sameer had had an injury.

The confusion on her face intensified. She darted to the phone like lightning and from that instant, with every passing moment our fear and grief magnified to unbearable proportions. Mr Puri sat silently by her side, supportive and strong, sharing her pain.

It was incomprehensible. Sameer had been here, with us just ten days ago, laughing, joking, enriching our lives with his energetic style. At a party hosted a few days before he had left, I had called in a stand-up artist and much to his embarrassment, no one had really laughed at his jokes. As the grim-faced guests watched, Sameer had taken the mike from him and for the next hour the entire party was in splits with his improvised humour.

Before leaving, he had taken on a hectic schedule of interviews for vacancies in the company.

'I will get back to you on my return,' he had said.

Having decided to start working in the company in addition to pursuing his music career, Sameer had visited his tailor Shamim and ordered a new set of business suits that now waited on hangers to be worn.

225

His music director Gaurav Dayal was confounded. Sameer had met him just before leaving and had finalized the details for his new album.

'I am starting on this the day I get back. I won't be long. Perhaps ten days,' he had assured Gaurav.

Today it all felt so unreal; it was like walking through another dimension.

My mother struggled, making phone calls, talking to doctors, calling every contact she thought could help. The Apollo air ambulance readied itself to fly Sameer back to proper medical care, until it was clear that now there was no urgency. The world ceased in that moment, there was silence within. Complete and utter silence, as though the music had abruptly stopped short.

Meher Apa flew down with her family to be by my mother's side. The last time she had come to be with 'Shunno', as she calls her, was when she was four and my grandmother had taken ill. Years later, she was there once again, knowing that today she was perhaps even more vulnerable.

Once again I think I was not able to grieve for my loss – holding on stoically to the family – but I will mourn him forever. My little brother, who sleeps warmly in my heart.

Summer Leads to Spring

It has been a while since Sameer left us. The air is turning warmer by the day; summer is descending on the city softly but steadily. My mother's staff is diligently planning her wardrobe and packing her bags for her vacation to her home in London and soon she will be away on a much needed break. It's been a trying time and through it all I have been by her side almost every waking hour. Where the tips of her fingers ended she always found mine, close at hand, assuring her that I was there for her.

It is hard to comprehend how profoundly Sameer's loss has touched our lives. In some ways we can never go back to being the same again, as carefree and light about life as we once were. Yet through this ultimate test we have emerged closer and stronger as a family; perhaps it was in our genes, or in our ancestors' blessings, that we, the children of Rahat Manzil, faced our worst tragedy with equanimity and courage.

Sharik became our biggest support in the months after Sameer's death as he handled the company with responsibility and grace, just as I had shouldered Shahnaz Herbals through my father's loss.

Zubek has formed a wonderful bond with my mother and they have become the best of friends, meeting for coffee at Barista and chatting about life as only my mother can. He tells her all about new technologies and how he plans to incorporate them in the company and she tries to help him find himself at an age when he enjoys wandering through the possibilities that life has to offer.

After the initial shock that left us numb I saw my mother harness her energies once again, till she was strong enough to visit Sameer's resting place in Patna.

As she lowered her head to touch the ground in prayer and her thoughts enveloped the memory of her son, she was startled by the click of a camera. At that moment she realized that even in her darkest hour, she was first and foremost a 'story'.

Troubled by the innumerable versions that she had heard about Sameer's death, she decided to visit the chief minister of Bihar and request him for an in-depth inquiry into her son's death.

The next few months were consumed in chasing versions that would dissolve into thin air; distance made it quite impossible to keep track of leads and with each passing day it seemed less likely that the facts would emerge, or that we would be able to recognize them if they ever did. I convinced my mother to let Sameer's memory rest in peace so that we could talk of him with ease and remember only the happiest times we had spent together as a family.

My mother returned to work with a new energy and today, Shahnaz Herbals is more than a company. It is hope itself, for my mother and for future generations. It is not about economics, it is about passion that brings together a family to work for a single purpose, a dream that has passed down from her to me and to my children and I hope to theirs too, one day.

With the introduction of the law banning the commercial use of residential properties, the salon at M-86, as well as the school, which was housed close by, was moved to its new premises. I was immersed in identifying the new address and designing the flagship salon of the future. Today when people walk in and say that they have rarely seen a salon, even in the most modern countries, with the look and feel of this new centre, it gives me immense satisfaction. Built on an entire floor in a glistening new shopping mall in Greater Kailash, Part II it was a challenge to live up to the plush elegance that was the hallmark of M-86 and combine it with a modern state-of-the-art feel. The offices are now at Nehru Place; I discovered a spectacular ninth-floor space where every window faces the serene grounds of the Lotus Temple built in pure white marble. From where I sit, on rainy days, I can see thunder flash in the sky and crackle past the solitary spiritual structure. When people walk in they just keep looking out of the window and it's hard to pull them back from the magnificent view. I smile in satisfaction because relocating the two most vital aspects of the company has proved to be a rewarding project.

In the future, I think spas and wellness are going to become a major part of our growth. The needs of the new, exhausted generation will require something more than the application of creams to brighten their faces. We will need to give them a dose of absolute calm and the prescribed 'homework' will need to include deep meditation and complete lifestyle changes. As always the research department is working hard to contribute innovations that will be industry landmarks like the 24-Carat Gold range.

As for me, I will continue to work on bringing out new products that I hope will make Shahnaz Herbals proud of its inventiveness and quality; products that will maintain our role as a frontrunner and innovator. I would like Shahnaz Herbals to challenge the future with growth and expansion. I would like to 'hold' my mother's dream and add my own dreams to it. I would definitely look at making a bid for an international presence in a larger way so that my mother's dream fills every conceivable space.

I would also like to expand myself to experience something beyond, follow my bliss for a while and write many more books. I believe that we need to extend our vision to the maximum, to touch, feel, celebrate the entire universe if one can. I don't believe in remaining trapped in a tight environment. Prisons are often of different kinds, not always concrete and sometimes we build them around ourselves. There is too much happening in the world and life's opportunities can't be a missed experience.

I was first introduced to social work by a precious friend, Ms. Jetsun Pema, His Holiness The Dalai Lama's sister and since my training centres for women have become a rewarding part of my life. Apart for my contribution to Shahnaz Herbals, I would like to be known as someone who made a difference to people's lives.

As evening falls on the city my mother's silver Rolls is seen gliding down the rush-hour roads to her favourite destination. Her love affair with Barista is well known by now and after a full day's work she essentially moves her base to the popular coffee shop and settles down there for the evening.

I often accompany her and after walking past the temptations of the glistening stores at Select Citywalk we make our way to the first floor which houses the huge open-plan Barista that has the ambience of a street café in Europe, or the closest one can get to the concept.

We sit down and relax for a while and then the factory heads join us for a recap of the day. The area turns into a workplace with a change of scene and a change of spirit too. Amidst the chatter and the cacophony, the fragrance of the aromatic beans, the sound and laughter, many company decisions are taken.

Every few minutes someone approaches the table for an autograph, a picture, or just an opportunity to tell my mother of their admiration for her. She waves out to friends and acquaintances as they pass by and are immediately invited to join in. Though Barista reserves her table in the evenings, the group constantly grows spilling onto nearby chairs.

A group of girl students from Kellogg's Business School who have opted to come to India to observe the company and its creator are sitting around their case study, their pencils and booklets in their hands, earnestly jotting down every word she says. As she speaks on of her near child marriage and her days of struggle, her climb to the top of the corporate ladder, the incredulity is clear on their faces. Meanwhile, Barista serves up coffee and flavoured iced teas and plates of snacks, some sent across to the security personnel who watch on carefully.

The little diary that she carries with her at all times is passed around to everyone present to write in its pages and sign it with the date and time. This diary is very important to my mother, because the many pages that have been filled in, chronicle her life in the words of different people who meet her. All the while the two personal cameramen that follow her every move have their cameras poised on her.

Some of her favourite stores are sending their latest arrivals for her to see and she is casually choosing the ones she likes. Her financial controller, who has been with the company from its inception, tries to slip away finding her absorbed in other things but she is quick to notice the movement. 'Don't leave as yet, Mr Malik. I want you to come down with me and select a handbag for your wife.'

The whole gathering then moves to the shops where she plays the perfect Santa Clause, getting her managers to try on shoes and jackets, picking out earrings and clothes for their wives, toys for the kids. My mother's love for shopping is rivalled by her desire for gifting. She rarely keeps what she buys and enjoys gifting like very few people I know. As the shopping bags pile up, the Barista waiter comes down with the mandatory box of cakes for every company executive to take home for their families.

The corporate professionals who join the company are often left confused by the exuberant excesses of their boss but they do realize that if it weren't for this personality trait there may have been no Shahnaz Herbals; that this is more than a company – this is an experience of an extraordinary kind.

My mother's Barista evenings need to be documented if only as part of company lore, because they define the signature style of functioning of its mentor – a style in which work and play merge, or perhaps one in which work never ceases, it just takes different forms.

Talking of playfulness, it is very serious business for my mum. She loves life with a passion that makes every moment tick twice. She multi-tasks, multi-revels, makes pleasure a part of every situation she can, unless of course the situation demands otherwise.

Franchisees from across the globe can often be seen in China Garden in Greater Kailash Part II having dinner with the family after a full evening at Citywalk and leave the country not just with a business plan but with Kashmiri carpets and innumerable mementos, having lived and received the complete Shahnaz Husain experience.

My relationship with my mother has constantly been changing through the years. She has mothered me and often I have mothered her. The best description came from Zila Khan, the Sufi singer who once came up to me at a party and said, 'Every family that makes it big has one pillar that supports it. I feel you are that pillar in your family.'

Nothing that anyone has ever said has made me feel nicer. Indeed, I do think my mother made it through with her determination and something more. Today my mother and I are two women, sometimes young girls, who chat, exchange notes, rely on each other and are the best of friends. Isn't that what a perfect relationship should be?

If all this sounds too idyllic, let me say, it is not. As the Vedas teach you, it is not that life will not give you problems, it will; it is your response to them and how you deal with them that defines your problems.

As I said, my mother is leaving for London soon. By the time she returns home the seasons will have changed and Delhi's weather will be turning pleasant and wonderful.

I would like to end this touching chapter of my mother's life with a quote from my favourite poet Pablo Neruda: *'You can cut all the flowers but you cannot keep Spring from coming.'*

Epilogue: A Leap in Time

It is like stepping into another time, beautifully preserved. There is history everywhere – on the high, painted ceilings, the embellished walls, the flowing drapes and carved furniture. It has never failed to raise my adrenaline to dangerous levels, the drive down the cobbled path with guards in livery, the car somehow always coming to a screeching halt at the exact spot, the doors flinging open magically. After clearing heavy security, you are led up to the stately corridors of Rashtrapati Bhavan in New Delhi.

A hush falls over the Ashoka Hall as President A.P.J. Abdul Kalam walks down the aisle between the seats and takes his place on the ceremonial chair. The bugles fade and the room suddenly echoes with the tune of the national anthem.

With every beat of the drums I feel my heart thump louder, intensifying the surreal feeling of walking into a page of history. I smile to share the moment with my family and see their faces beaming with pride and emotion. A separate row of chairs is placed in front, occupied by men and a few women of various ages. They are the best and brightest in their fields and the occasion is to honour their contribution to the country.

'Shahnaz Husain, for her contribution to Ayurveda.'

The words ring out in the room and as I watch my mother rise and elegantly walk up to the President of India to receive one of the highest civilian honours of the country, the Padmashree, I have tears of happiness in my eyes. She has crossed the magical line of success to a place where commerce is secondary and achievement is akin to national pride. She has made her family, her friends, her company and loved ones proud and, most importantly, she has made her country proud.

I look up and smile silently, thanking the two men who I know she is thinking of too: my grandfather who always believed in her and encouraged her to find her identity and my father who shared her life and her trials and supported her throughout her journey to the top. They are here too, watching her at the pinnacle of success and cheering her on.

As I finish her story, I realize how little had ever been said about her.

Who is this beautiful, brilliant woman? Where did she come from? What made her become what she is today?

For me this book is a promise kept.

'Write a book on me, Nelofar,' she had said to the hissing of the coffee machine in Barista.

Well, I did, Mum.

I sat down to write a book on you but it turned out to be much more than just a book. It has turned out to be a treasure of timeless memories, some good, some bad; it is the story of your dreams and a testament to your struggle; a record of a life lived with love, heartbreak, passion and above all, with unwavering faith.

Tomorrow, if things change, *when* things change, this much will still be true. My promise kept to you, dear Mum.